Of Pitfalls and Pratfalls

A Story of the Trials and Tribulations of Growing Up

Dorothy F. Hart

With appreciation to
Colin Carrie, M.P. for
Oshawa and his
dedicated staff.
2023.
Dorothy F. Hart.

 FriesenPress

Suite 300 - 990 Fort St
Victoria, BC, V8V 3K2
Canada

www.friesenpress.com

Gordon Hart - Translator

ISBN
978-1-03-911084-7 (Hardcover)
978-1-03-911083-0 (Paperback)
978-1-03-911085-4 (eBook)

1. BIOGRAPHY & AUTOBIOGRAPHY, PERSONAL MEMOIRS

Distributed to the trade by The Ingram Book Company

For my grandchildren.
Cherish the memories of your youth.

Steven and Jacquiline Hachie
b- 1994, b-1990

Kyle, Trevor and Nicholas Hachie
b- 1991, b- 1994, b- 1997

Gillian and Kristian Nese
b-2003, b- 2005

Great Grandson
Benjamin Forrest
b- 2012

Chapter 1

The Beginning

On April 7, 1943, my twin brother, David, and I entered this world with a bang-literally! We were born during an air raid in Scotland. The world was at war! The story we were told was that we were delivered by nuns in a location other than a hospital. As I understand, nuns and midwifes set up nurseries in chapels and church basements to care for new mothers and infants, as the hospitals were fully occupied by injured survivors of bombings.

Our Christening at Arborfield, England

After Our Christening at Arborfield, England

And at that time, our parents were basically strangers to us. Dad was away, fighting for our freedom, and Mom worked in a munitions factory in Glasgow to support the home front, as most able-bodied women did at this time.

Our grandparents, Grandpa and Gaga, were given the task of raising us. Grandpa took charge of David, and Gaga looked after my needs. Our home was a beautiful Victorian house in the quaint city of Stirling. For the most part, David slept with Grandpa and I crawled into bed with Gaga. She would use a long-handled bed warmer, heated by a fire in the bedroom fireplace, to warm the bed, making it cozy. I often watched her brush and braid her long hair, then put on her nightcap. Her dentures were put into a glass of water on the bedside table.

There was a large garden at the back of the house, surrounded by a large stone wall. A big wooden door at the end of the stone path leading to the front yard gave us a comforting feeling of safety. The path was lined with tall pines that emitted a sweet smell after one of Scotland's many rain showers. The garden itself had fruit trees, a large variety of berries and shrubs, and a pond surrounded by a rock garden. The rock garden was covered by little strawberries and was the private area for David and me.

In our pram in the back garden in Stirling, Scotland

Across from our house was a large area that had once been a lot of houses. They were all completely destroyed by bombs. The area had been cleared and divided into small plots of land, and each plot was allotted to the homes surrounding the devastation. Grandpa had the first plot because our house had been nearest the destruction. He built a greenhouse for growing tomatoes that had the delicious smell and warmth of heaven.

Other vegetables (although tomatoes are not a vegetable), such as cabbage, lettuce, peas, beans, and carrots, grew in abundance in the rest of our area. A larger area was designated for potatoes. There was always enough growing to share with friends and neighbours and anyone in need. Food was quite scarce at times, and not everyone had the ability to grow their own. Gaga canned and made preserves with everything we grew. I got to observe, learn, and help. I became quite adept at shelling peas. We never went hungry.

Grandpa (John Blyth Forgan 1885-1965)
Gaga (Elizabeth M. Forgan nee Logan 1887-1960)

Gaga taught me much about preserving and cooking, although I wasn't allowed to actually use the large gas cooker. However, I was entrusted to stir the laundry that had been put into a big tub in the corner of the kitchen. I did have to stand on a footstool to reach. A fire underneath the tub heated the water almost to boiling, and lye was poured in to clean the sheets and clothes. I would use a large pole to agitate everything and then pull it all out and drop it into a big basin. We then carried the basin to the mangle room, which consisted of two huge rollers the length of a large folded sheet. One by one, the wash was put into the rollers and squeezed through by a big handle that took all the water out. All the clean laundry was then taken outside and hung up on the clothesline to dry. Once dry, items were brought inside to be pressed. I learned to take a flat iron out of the little shelf in the hot fireplace in the sitting room and spit on the flat side to determine it was hot enough to iron the clothes and sheets. A sizzle was good!

On nice sunny days, David and I would help bring all the area rugs outside to hang them on the clothesline. Our job was to beat the rugs with tools that looked like tennis rackets. We would pound away amid clouds of dust and debris from everyone who walked on them, and we'd usually end upon the grass, rolling with laughter. Of course, a bath always followed.

Growing up wasn't all work. We often walked into town, where Grandpa had a small clock workshop off a courtyard on a second floor. There was a dairy on one end of the yard. Horses pulling wagons of milk cans clip clopped on the cobblestones, trying to avoid the many cats trying to lap up any spilled milk. Grandpa would repair old clocks and watches, and his little office tick-tocked loudly the sound echoed through the courtyard.

Across the street was a music shop owned by Grandpa and one of his brothers. David and I were allowed to have any musical instrument as long as we could carry it. Obviously, that left out pianos. I remember I got a lovely tambourine and David, a harmonica.

We sometimes went to the Stirling Golf and Country Club, situated beneath the glorious Stirling Castle. Grandpa was their golf pro, and our family was known as the originators of the famous Forgan golf clubs. For many generations, the golf clubs were known as the best in Britain.

Grandpa had many talents. He could play any musical instrument just by listening to it first. He collected many unusual items; some were from South Africa and Asia. I remember a very long horn-like instrument that he told me took five men to hold it up just to play. He wrote music, was an inventor, and held patents on many items used at the time. Some things used today, centuries later, have been adapted from his inventions, like the moped, sock trees, and the scooter. He could fix grandfather clocks, tune pianos, and was still capable of raising two mischievous youngsters like us.

Grandpa (John Blyth Forgan)

Gaga and Grandpa had as certain number of rules for us to follow. One rule was that we weren't allowed to remove the sign, if present, on the back of the toilet that said, "Do not use." It meant that the wooden toilet seat had just been varnished, and if we sat down, we would not be able to get back up. That was actually true, as I speak from experience. Another rule was that we weren't allowed to push other children that we took a dislike to into the backyard pond. There was a particularly annoying whinny little girl about our age that visited Gaga with her parents. We were instructed to take her outside to play. She was inclined to have temper tantrums if she didn't get her own way, so we gave her a gentle little push into the pond to cool her off. Luckily, Gaga was in the kitchen making tea and saw us out the window. The child was rescued and taken indoors to dry up. No one was sure if it was an accident, but the little child came back outside and very smugly modelled her new dry clothes—my favourite pink party dress with the lace collar. I felt that the punishment for nearly drowning her was too extreme!

My favourite pink party dress

Grandpa was also given rules by Gaga. He wasn't allowed to eat his breakfast at the family table because he insisted on putting a spoonful of sugar on his porridge. That was considered a disgusting habit and a blatant disrespect for Scottish etiquette.

At the back corner of the garden, among the fruit trees, was a small summer house. It had no windows but a peaked roof that was opened at the top. It was an eerie place that David and I liked to play in. The little house was very warm, had a strange odour about it, and things like flags were suspended from the ceiling. Many years later, I learned that Grandpa used the little house as a drying room for tobacco that he grew in the garden plot.

Some smells and sounds elicit strong memories. The sweet smell of pine trees after a rain shower in summer still gives me delight. On the other hand, I remember the musty odour and discomfort we endured from gas masks that we had to wear during an air raid. I still get chills when I hear that noise. My earliest memory is of my brother and I sitting in our pram, getting excited because my mother was taking us out for a walk after days of rain had kept us housebound. I remember Gaga standing on the back door steps, Mom opening the big wooden door, and the sound of the sirens screaming through the air. I can see Gaga running down the stairs, grabbing David from the pram, and Mom slamming the wooden door and trying to get me out of the pram. I was hanging onto the handle, and she dragged me and the pram halfway up the stairs before she could get me inside to the safety of our shelter under the front stairs. I remember the sound of drones overhead. Planes flying in formation were an indication for everyone to run inside immediately to seek shelter.

Every window in the house had long heavy black velvet curtains to keep light from leaking out. The curtains were kept drawn in rooms not being used at the time. At night, they were closed tight, and people called watchers would check all the homes, looking for any slivers of light that would give the position or location of towns. Only spies would give the enemy a target. There were tall gas lights along the streets, and if the air raid sirens sounded, a designated person, with a very long pole, would immediately run to each lamp and snuff out the gas flame.

Gaga was a very wise woman. She claimed that some of her skills were attributed to the *Ladies' Home Journal,* a magazine with bountiful information on running a household. Among the pages was a description of the common ailment called the Victorian faint. The faint was due to young ladies of the era lacing up their corsets too tightly to look slimmer. Sometimes a few ribs were broken, but more commonly, their airways were constricted, causing them to faint. Gaga always carried a little enamel box filled with snuff. A little pinch of snuff under the nose usually revived her abruptly. Sometimes, I saw her taking a little snuff herself after an exhausting day of cleaning, cooking, and washing. A couple of times a month, my mother would be home and cook the family dinner. Dinner usually was a concoction of dried milk and fried fish. I had a distinct dislike for it and usually told everyone I was feeling sick. When I was ill, I was always made to lie down and a mustard plaster was applied to my chest to supposedly sweep out impurities. My alternative for refusing to eat my meal was to hold my breath, then promptly fall to the floor. Gaga said it was the Victorian faint, and I was given a pinch of snuff up my nose. Although I was never required to wear corsets, I faulted my mother's cooking. Today, my behaviour would be considered a temper tantrum and I would have been sent to my room! And it was at least fifty years before I ever ate fish again, unless it came in a can.

Dad British submarine service (Robert William Hannah Jack 1913-2008)

On May 1945, the war in Europe was over. On September 2, 1945, Japan surrendered. World War Two was over. It was a time to celebrate. Most of the soldiers came home, but my father was delayed for a few more years. Originally, he had been in the British Royal Navy Submarine Service, but after an episode with a burst appendix, he was released from the service. He transferred to the British India units fighting the Japanese, on the Burma Road in India. With the end of the war, he was sent to Japan to oversee the closure of munitions factories and the like.

When the time for him to come home finally arrived, Grandpa and Gaga decided that David and I should be the ones to greet him first. We were instructed to answer the door while the rest of family stayed back. We were unsure of how we would know what he looked like but were assured he would be wearing a uniform. We were excited when the doorbell rang and anxious to welcome our father. Our daddy was home!

Major Robert W.H. Jack, British India Army

After a short wait, our grandparents and mother came down the hall to be greeted by David clutching one leg and me the other, yelling "Welcome home, Daddy." The look on the postman's face was sheer horror!

Uncle Dae also returned to the family home after serving in Egypt and Germany. He was an avid photographer and even had his own darkroom, just off the main sitting room. Of course, David and I were prime targets for his camera.

Prime targets for Uncle Dae

He also had an interesting hobby of collecting butterflies. In the upstairs hall of our grandparents' home, there was a large glass display case with many exotic butterflies collected from Europe and Africa. Different sizes, shapes, and colours were awe inspiring. He also spent many hours creating fancy fly-fishing hooks, using a huge variety of colourful feathers. I often wondered where he found such pretty bird's willing to donate their feathers. His fancy hooks were obviously successful as he frequently came home with trout from the highland brooks.

Upstairs in the house was a large sitting room. From what I observed, it was only used when Gaga had her lady friends visiting, and they would play the game of bridge and drink tea. On the wall across from the stairs, adjacent to the upstairs landing, there was a collection of animal heads, most bigger than us. There was a good selection of gazelles, water buffalo, rhinos, and a lion, as well as other species from Africa. Grandpa's family had lived in South Africa and Kenya when he was a boy. They return to Scotland just before the Boer War, a fight between African natives and white landowners. I now understand the sign over the front door of our house. Printed in red, on the large glass window over the door, were the letters "RUARAKA."

Grandpa and Gaga on the steps of Ruaraka

As an adult, I asked Dad what it meant. He replied, "Whore house in Swahili, an African dialect." However, doing some research, I found out that it was the trade name for Kenya Breweries Limited and actually means "beer and ale," another word for "inn."

At the end two doors away of our street was a large stadium, as well as tennis courts. On weekends, there was often a football game being played and hordes of fans, with their bright colored scarves, would walk past our house on their way to a game. David and I would take to sitting on the wall surrounding the front of the house and wave and smile at the very happy patrons. Often, they would throw coins at us. And after they had all passed by, we would go to a little store at the corner that sold ice cream; we usually had amassed enough coins to buy cones. We deduced that it paid to be small, friendly, and charming!

After Dad came home, we sometimes would wade in one of the many lochs and picnic in the Highlands. Mom would bring all the fixings to make sandwiches on the little beach. I learned to love the salty taste of sand in the cucumber sandwiches, and once we were out of the water, she would check your legs for leeches. A sprinkle of salt on their tails would release their hold from our skin.

Fortunately, there are no mosquitoes in Scotland, although clouds of midges are plentiful. It doesn't take long to remember to keep your mouth shut if you happen to walk into a cloud of the pesky insects. Luckily, they never fly alone, so it's easier to avoid them and they don't seem to follow you around either.

In Scotland, Christmas is mainly for the children. Hogmanay (New Year's Eve) was a holiday everyone celebrates, as long as they can stay awake long enough.

On that day, David and I were given a small glass of ginger beer. We thought we were drinking alcohol. We all ate Scottish shortbread while waiting for the clock to chime at midnight to welcome in the New Year. We were allowed to stay up until the first foot arrived. The first foot was always identified as a tall dark-haired man who would present Grandpa with a lump of coal to bring good luck to the New Year. We would all wait in anticipation for the visitor after toasting the New Year. Uncle Dae was not allowed to be a first foot because he had red hair, and red hair was considered bad luck.

Uncle Dae and Mom

Chapter 2

Glasgow

When David and I were five, with Dad now in the picture, we moved about twenty miles from Stirling to Glasgow. Our sister Diana soon arrived sometime in the middle of the night on September 27, 1948. Babies were usually born at home, and I vividly remember Dad waking David and me up to introduce our new sister. I did a quick glance at the child and immediately ran to the window to catch a glimpse of the stork leaving. Obviously, I wasn't abreast of how babies were born and was of the firm belief that they arrived via the stork delivery.

Storks were a common bird in Scotland, particularly noted for sitting in large nests on top of chimneys. They are very large birds and inclined to make a lot of mess. When their nests were abandoned, once a year, the chimney sweeps would arrive, the furniture in our sitting room would be covered with large cloths, and the flue would be swept of assorted branches and an abundance of bird droppings.

Diana in the backyard of 113 Norse Rd. Glasgow

It was not wise to remain in the room during the cleaning process. Soot does indeed get into the nose and eyes—usually an observation made only once!

In Britain, the school year starts at age five. David and I settled in at a large school, half a block from home. Many neighbours had a cinder lane running behind all the backyards and lined with backyard gates. There was an occasional garage entrance, but I don't ever remember seeing any cars using the lanes. At the end of our lane was the school and schoolyard, which was surrounded by a tall iron fence just across the main road. It was easy to find our way around on most days. Frequently, a heavy fog took over the skies and you could not see your outstretched hands. Police would arrive on those days, waving large lanterns so we could find the schoolyard entrance. Once we exited, there was no worry about cars crossing the road because all driving abruptly stopped during heavy fog days. We found our way home by counting gates along the back lanes.

Not far from our house was Victoria Park: a beautiful scenic park with a pond where David could sail his little boat. Close by, there was also an underground Petrified Forest. It had a large glass window above ground that we can look down into and see parts of the display. We could see tall trees made of stone and visitors walking below; those were the paying public. On our way to the park, we had to cross a railway bridge. We would sit on the stonewall and wait for the steam engines passing beneath us. The engineers would always wave and blow their whistles, and billows of smoke would waft over as.

Across from the school was a church. During the week of school days, they served a breakfast to children who hadn't eaten at their homes. Most of the children came from the dock tenements and were mostly from poor families. Their mothers would leave home very early to do laundry and housekeeping for better off families, and if they had a father, he would be working even longer hours on the docks. Glasgow had a large shipyard on the Clyde River and was known as for its shipbuilders throughout the world. At lunchtime, the children were given lunch. On a few occasions, Mom and Diana would be away during the lunch hour and she would buy a ticket for us to get lunch at the church. Obviously, the regulars didn't pay. The basin of the church was close to a scene from the Charles Dickens novel *Oliver Twist:* long tables and benches, custodians calling for quiet while serving, what David and I called, inedible food. A fast rule was our plates had to be cleaned (eaten) or we wouldn't get the dessert. Dessert was usually a dry dollop of tapioca that I swear look like fish eyes. Many years passed before I actually enjoyed a bowl of creamy tapioca. Fortunately, there was always a child sitting next to us that was happy to clean our plates.

On weekends in the summer, the church hosted a lot of weddings. Many of the neighbourhood children, including us, would wait outside the church doors for the wedding party to exit. Large wealthier families and guests would toss coins and confetti at the newlyweds. Depending on how happy everyone was, we often found half pennies, pennies, and the odd threepence or sixpence—usually enough to pay for a movie, always a double feature with a serial that left you hanging, a cartoon, and a newsreel.

Because Dad was home on weekends, our parents would take the opportunity to sleep in. We, on the other hand, were more inclined to get up and running. To keep us in bed longer, Mom would put a plate of fresh fruit and some biscuits beside our beds for the next morning before she settled for the night. This was supposed to keep us occupied. We, however, would frequently wake up early in the dark and start eating are treats and comparing our goodies. One early morning, I was delighted to find a nice apple and took a big bite. It didn't quite taste right, so I left it unfinished. In the daylight, I saw a half worm sticking out of the apple right where I had bitten. I knew what had happened to the other half. That was the last time we ate snacks in the dark.

First picnic with Dad in the Highlands

One Sunday, we went to visit Dad's aunts. We called them "the sweetie aunts." They were two elderly spinsters who lived together and owned and operated the sweet shop, making and selling every kind of candy imaginable. They lived in a lovely flat (apartment) above their store and took David and me downstairs to taste test the goodies. They also made us a poke of candy to take with us. Sweets were very hard to come by at that time, as everyone was allowed only a certain number of coupons to purchase basic necessities. Candies and sweets were usually not on the list.

Another trip we made was to Edinburgh to see a special performance of *Peter Pan* on stage. Peter was played by the most famous actor of the time, Mary Martin. Her portrayal of Peter is legendary. Tinkerbell was played by a little spotlight that danced around the stage. During the epic scene where the little fairy is poisoned, Peter asked us children in the audience to yell at the top of our lungs to save Tinkerbell's life. We had to shout "I believe in fairies." Everyone was literally screaming so loudly; it was a wonder the roof of the theater didn't cave in. But we had saved Tinkerbell! We also went home with sore throats.

During the week, Dad would leave for work in the morning before we got out of bed. Mom, of course, would be up early to prepare breakfast and light the fire in the sitting room to warm the house. Our underwear was often on the fireplace screen to warm on a cold and damp mornings. David and I would go outside to play or go to school. We had to get out of the way for the maid to do her usual cleanup. On some rainy evenings, we would play indoors, acting out our favourite story, *The Tortoise and the Hare,* and taking turns at each roll. Every evening, we would sit around the fire while Mom read a chapter from one of our favourite books, like *Alice in Wonderland,* before going to bed, which was before Dad got home from work. He and Mom always ate later and said they needed the peace and quiet.

Most weekends, Dad would get the car, and David and I would climb into the back seat. We would all drive to Stirling to spend the weekend with Grandpa and Gaga while Mom, Dad, and Diana went off somewhere else. Occasionally, we would go on a picnic or visit Dad's mother, we called her "Granny." She looked remarkably like the portrait of Whistler's Mother that I had seen in a picture book. She always set a huge table with all sorts of cakes, sponges, pastries, and puddings. David would taste every item of the sweet goodies and always ended up with a stomach ache afterwards. I can still hear Granny saying, "Leave the wee bairn alone" to Mom and Dad after they scolded him for eating too much.

Uncle Wilson and Aunt Betty

Sometimes Aunt Betty, Uncle Wilson, who was Dad's brother, and our two cousins, Frances (my age) and Doreen (Diana's age) would come for a visit. They travelled from London, England, where they lived. On one visit, I had just got my first two-wheel bicycle, and Dad and Uncle Wilson decided they were going to teach me how to ride it. They took turns pushing me from behind on the back lane until I was able to stay up right. All bicycles in Scotland have hand brakes, and I had to try and remember which brake worked the back and which worked the front wheel. I finally managed to stay up, riding like mad, leaving my instructors behind. I couldn't remember which break to press, so I kept going on the sidewalk around the whole block until I arrived back on the cinder lane behind our house. At that point, everyone was yelling at me to brake. Naturally, I pressed the wrong side and abruptly stopped the bike. Unfortunately, I didn't stop, going over the handlebars headfirst into the cinders. I still have the grey scar on my elbow as evidence.

I wasn't the only disaster walking on two feet. David has some major moments also. He was always climbing and, one day, decided to "hop over" an old iron railing, instead of going over a low wall. There was a fancy filigree work with spikes at the top, and he managed to become impaled in the groin. He spent some time in the hospital and recovered nicely, however, lost a small body part that only boys like to brag about. A decade later, he used his loss to advantage by betting his schoolmates that unlike them, he was only endowed with one. He dropped his pants to prove his statement and collected money for losing their bets. The first entrepreneur in our family.

At the foot of our backyard was a pretty flower garden bordered by the laneway fence. There was a shed at the corner of the garden partially covered by a large Rowan tree. I spent many hours huddled in the corner, shaded by the tree and shed, watching for the fairies to appear among the flowers in the garden. Everyone knows that fairies like gardens but are very secretive and don't like being watched. I had noticed a fairy ring (a circle of mushrooms) close by, so I knew there was a good chance they would visit my garden. I would lay very quietly every day, for hours on end, afraid to blink or move a limb. When the flowers started to fade and the day's shortened and cooled, I started to think I had missed them. There was always next year!

As children, we enjoyed the holidays. Christmas was always at the top of our list. On Christmas Eve, we would stand around the decorated tree, and Dad would carefully light the little candles that had been pinned to the branches. Obviously, we weren't allowed to be near the tree and it was never left lit without a lot of supervision. We would hang our stockings on the mantel to wait for Santa's visit, and amazingly, the filled stockings would be at the bottom of our beds on Christmas morning.

Halloween was always fun too. David and I would dress up and parade to our doctor's house. They were my parent's best friends. We would be invited in and had to entertain their friends before we could receive our goodies, usually cakes or tarts—a sort of "sing for your supper." Though completely tone deaf, David usually sang a nursery rhyme, and I would recite a poem. We didn't stay long because we would rush home to greet our guests. Usually, the ones trick or treating in full costume would come into the house and entertain us by singing, dancing, or acting out a short play, and then they would sit down to a meal of cakes, desserts, and sweets. Sometimes, they would come in pairs but, other times, in large groups. Most were college or university students. Smaller or younger children didn't really participate and were more entertained. Since there were no pumpkins in Britain, we were allowed to carve turnips or make paper lanterns to hang over the door.

Guy Fawkes Night, which is November 5, was great fun. We would spend time helping to make an effigy of Guy Fawkes, the Catholic traitor who tried to kill King James the VI of Scotland in 1605. Usually, there was one made for each street. Guy would be hoisted up onto a big pile of logs and sticks and then set ablaze. After the fire and Guy were extinguished, the adults would celebrate with punch and eggnog, and we had to go to bed.

Easter preparations started a week early. Mom would hoard the eggs for several weeks, as only a limited number was doled out with coupons. The eggs were boiled with the hope they weren't rotten. Out of a dozen eggs, we were lucky to get six safe enough to eat. A rotten egg smells like sulphur and smells up the whole house. Mom would make different dyes (no idea with what), and we would paint our eggs for Easter morning. We would take them outside to a nearby hill and roll them down, hoping to break everyone's but not your own. Fingers were crossed that we would get an egg that wasn't rotten. We would get to then eat our eggs—a real treat when eggs were so scarce.

In 1951, Dad left us to come to Canada so we could start a new life. He had travelled extensively throughout the world and was familiar with the standards and policies of governments. He particularly wanted a British colony and settled on Australia or Canada. My mother's cousin David Forgan lived in Toronto with his family and was well established. He sponsored Dad, and the choice of country was decided. Mom also had an elderly aunt and cousins living in Alberta. It was settled that Dad would find a job and a home for us while Mom would sell the house, pack our belongings, and get the paperwork sorted before joining Dad a year later.

Our school teacher was told about our plans to immigrate to Canada and decided on a geography lesson for our classmates. Maps of Canada were produced, and we learned about the people and customs of our soon-to-be new home. We found out about First Nations People and Inuit (not in those terms, though) and the fact that there was a lot of snow that really lasted all winter. We were sure that our house would be either an igloo or teepee.

Getting permission to travel was an ordeal. We all had to wait in a very crowded corridor of a building with hundreds of families getting permission to immigrate. We were all given physical checkups and smallpox vaccines and had our pictures taken for passports, although our photos never did appear on Mom's passport. We were only identified as "mother with three children."

The year 1952 was exceptionally busy preparing for our departure. On February 6, we were having our breakfast in the sitting room and listing to the radio. The broadcast was abruptly interrupted by a newscast announcing, "The King is dead . . . Long live the Queen." Britain's King George VI had just passed away and Princess Elizabeth was now our queen. They said she was in Africa at the tree house. It was many years before I found out it was the name of a hotel (Treetops Hotel), and that she wasn't actually sitting up in a child's playhouse!

Sorting all our toys was very hard. We were told that we could take all our books and one of our toys plus we could carry one. I packed my doll's bed made by Grandpa and carried my doll, dressed in a kilt. Everything else was to be donated to charity. David had a pet tortoise he had named Tommy. He was told that Tommy and also our goldfish could not, come on our boat. Grandpa told him that he knew a little boy who was very ill and couldn't get out of bed and would give a good and loving home for his pet. David reluctantly gave up Tommy but was quite upset when he found out that the little boy was 17. The goldfish were put into the little pond in Grandpa's garden we had often played around. A couple of years later, Gaga sent a photo of our two little goldfish. They were over a foot long, having grown into their environment. Fortunately, Grandpa was able to visit us in Canada after Gaga passed away. David did return to Scotland after he married; I didn't.

The house was sold, and the couple moved into the house with us for a month until we left for Canada. I thought it odd that they only had suitcases. They had bought all of our furniture, so we ended up with only suitcases and a large trunk containing our linens, kitchen items, and china. We spent our last few weeks in Stirling, saying goodbyes, before heading to England where we would catch the ship docked in Liverpool.

Ready to leave Scotland

Chapter 3

Canada, Here We Come!

In July 1952, we set sail for Canada on the HMS Franconia, Cunard Line. The ship was very large. Standing on the dock, we could not see the other end. After locating our compact room on board, David and I set out to explore. Our exploring was cut rather short, though, as we spent the first three days in our bunks with a severe case of seasickness, missing out on our departure from Britain. When we eventually got our sea legs, we found amazing areas of the ship where we could explore. Countless people willing to show us how things worked and the number of life forms in the ocean surrounding us, such as giant manta rays sunning themselves like huge red balloons on the surface.

We spotted icebergs in the distance and realized that the noise of the engines had changed: we had slowed down. Everyone appeared somewhat anxious. In April of 1912, the *Titanic* struck an iceberg and sunk, with 2435 lives lost. We were now sailing the same North Atlantic route to the new world. For days, the ship sailed at a crawl. Night and day, everyone had to wear heavy, awkward life jackets. Three times a day, the whistle would blow for everyone to line up on deck next to the lifeboats on each level for drill and were given instructions in case the alarm would sound. We saw the tips of many icebergs that seemed far away but, in reality, were mere feet away from the side of the ship, as we could see they extended out underwater. Crew members were constantly running up and down the decks, staring over the railings into the sea. We were assured that there were enough lifeboats to accommodate the over one thousand passengers on board. It was interesting to watch the lifeboats in operation, although I never got to sit in one. To David and me, it was just an adventure.

Due to the heavy iceberg invasion, the ship was over a week late, finally arriving just north of Newfoundland before entering the Saint Lawrence River. At times, the river was quite narrow and we could almost touch land on both sides of the large ship. The land itself seemed divided into hundreds of long strips, each separated by rocks or small hedgerow. Farmers would frequently wave at us. When the ship's engines stopped, a tiny little tugboat towed us to the docks at Quebec City. We could go no further because the channel was too narrow for our size.

We watched the unloading of all the cargo onto the docks and even saw the large green chest that was stuffed with all our linens, china, and a multitude of odds and ends. Just as the chest was being lowered onto the dock, the rigging gave way and it fell onto the dock. That explains why I only have half a set of Wedgwood dishes!

While waiting for passports and immigration papers to be processed, we sat in a large comfortable ships lounge. Mom had met an American woman with two children our age, who was returning home after visiting relatives in Britain. She asked us if we would like a Coke. This was a drink we were not familiar with, so we were anxious to try something new. After the first taste, we were convinced the Americans were trying to poison us! To this day, I will only drink a Coke float or rum with Coke.

When we were ready to disembark, we wound up on deck and observed hundreds of people all waving from shore. Pointing to the huge crowd below, Mom told David and me to wave to Daddy. We started to waive frantically when I asked David which one of those people was Daddy. He replied, "I don't know, just keep waving!"

Finally, after disembarking, greetings and hugs were over, Dad took us to a taxi stand to get transportation to the train station in Quebec City. We were to travel to Toronto by train to our new home. The taxi ride was horrifying, and David and I were yelling that we were going to crash because the driver was on the wrong side of the road. All the cars were driving on the wrong side of the road! We finally stopped at a small café because Mom wanted a cup of tea. Mom spoke French but found the French spoken in Quebec was only a tad similar to the real French spoken in France. She thought it was a lower-class dialect; when the waitress brought a cup of hot water and a little bag with a string attached, Mom exclaimed, "I would like a real cup of tea." The girl picked up the string and dangled the little bag into the hot water. My mother was mortified and said she was ready to go back to civilization in Scotland.

Arriving at our new home in Toronto was so exciting. We did get quite a scare while exploring the house. The basement had a large monster, with a gaping mouth, in one corner. We resolved to never enter that domain again. Winter was even worse, as the monster would wake up, groan loudly, and blow fire from the gaping mouth.

David and I shared a small bedroom upstairs, with too little cots. Our first night was very uncomfortable. We weren't told that Canada actually had a summer, and we were introduced to a heat wave. All our clothes were still packed, so we were wearing our heavy woolen kilts, sweater sets, and knee-high socks. We spent our night in our underwear, hoping our belongings would arrive from the ship by the following day. During our first night, we were wakened by something fluttering and squeaking over our heads and started screaming. Dad ran into the room and quickly shooed a bat out of the small area at the bottom of the window where he removed a little screen. Our hope was that bears or some other wild creature would not invade our home.

The school we were to attend was only a few doors from our house on Torrance Avenue. The principal told Mom that we were too young to go into Grade 5 so we were put into a Grade 4 class. The teachers thought we were very bright, not knowing the Grade 4 work was similar to our teachings already completed in Scotland.

A little girl that I had become friends with and who lived only two doors from our house had a television set. This was a relatively new invention, and her family had the only set on the street. She was allowed to invite one friend from school, and because I was a stranger to the country, as they were originally from China, I was frequently given this privilege. I was introduced to *Howdy Doody* and *Buffalo Bill*.

This strange country had many surprises. Back home, our houses were heated by fireplaces in each room, our food was kept cool by shopping daily, and perishables were put into buckets in the cooler basements. But in Canada, we were fortunate to have a refrigerator, another new invention. The other houses on the street all had iceboxes in their kitchen, and every week a wagon loaded with giant ice cubes would deliver large chunks of ice to each home to refill their iceboxes. Our refrigerator made its own ice, and weekly, we had to put bowls of hot water into the little freezer compartment at the top to melt the snow and ice off the sides to make room for the meats and anything else that required preserving for longer periods.

Language was a problem at times. Other children thought I talked funny and didn't know what a "pram" was. A "girdle" was something that overweight women wore, and Mom was embarrassed when she found herself in a hardware store looking for what Canadians called a "griddle." In school, we were taught Spanish because it was more popular for people to travel to the United States where English and Spanish were more common. French language, such as it was, was only used in Quebec at the time.

Dad finally bought us our own television set, and there were only two channels: one from Buffalo, New York, and the other broadcast from Rochester, New York. Mom became addicted to something called a "soap opera." The correlation with the name escapes me! We learned all about "cowboys and Indians" by watching *The Lone Ranger, The Roy Rogers Show, Hopalong Cassidy,* and *Red Ryder,* as well as numerous other westerns. At the time, we deduced that "cowboys and Indians" must only reside in Western Canada and the United States because we hadn't actually spied any in our vicinity.

We got to meet our Canadian relatives. Mom's cousin David Forgan, his wife, Helen, and two daughters, Mimi and Barbara, lived in Toronto. Uncle David, as we called him, had sponsored us to come to Canada and invited us to our very first Thanksgiving dinner. Our first taste of roast Turkey, stuffing, and cranberries was amazing. The only game birds we ever heard of were duck or goose. Pumpkin pie was very unusual in taste and texture but would become a favourite in later years. Uncle David had Parkinson's disease, so he had a problem with controlling his shaking hand. He was assigned to carve the turkey, and our hearts were in our mouths watching him tackle the bird with a large carving knife. When he poured the tea at the end of the meal, he missed most of the cup. David and I found it quite amusing and caught a case of giggles. Luckily, nobody seemed to notice or at least mentioned our behaviour.

After dinner, Cousin Mimi took me for a walk. They lived in Forest Hill, and their house bordered a forest. We went through a gate at the foot of the back garden and followed the little path through the dense woods. Mimi said she had a surprise for me. We trampled through the autumn leaves, admiring the beauty and sweet smell of fall, when suddenly we came to a tiny cottage nestled in the dense brush. Mimi knocked on the door and a hunched-over very old woman greeted us with a smile. I was immediately reminded of the tale of "Hansel and Gretel" at the old witch's lair. We were graciously ushered into the neat little house's cozy living room. We were given mugs of hot chocolate and delicious homemade cookies. The pleasant old lady wanted to know about Scotland, as I believe she had had family there many years ago. We had a delightful visit, and Mimi told me that she would often go to the little house to give the woman some company in her golden years.

Chapter 4

Country Living

After a year living in Toronto, we moved to a house in the outskirts of Whitby. It was closer to Dad's commute to work in Oshawa. Just off Highway 12, there were only a few houses on Hillcourt Avenue: large lots, well water, and plenty of fresh air. Around our little street, there were apple orchards, sand pits, and forests among farmer's fields, as well as friendly neighbours and plenty of cows.

Just after moving into our new old house, Dad brought a tiny kitten home, one of many kept in the basement of the factory where he worked to keep the mouse population at bay. The kitten was quite wild and not used to human contact. The first thing the little bundle of grey fur did was scramble up the sheer curtains in the living room, claws out, which Mom was in the process of hanging. In spite of my mother's wrath, the cat (named Neko) actually survived to a ripe old age of twenty, although I can't say the same for the curtains.

Neko and Bimbo

We also acquired a little beagle puppy we named Bimbo. He liked to run in the fields and often gently brought home baby rabbits (more likely hares) in his mouth. Because of that, Dad and David built rabbit hutches in the backyard to keep them safe until they were fully grown, when we released them into the woods at the end of our little street.

1954 was a memorable year, not only for us as newcomers but also for the history of Canada. Like many new immigrants, we were anxious to see and explore this fabulous country. Our first trip was naturally to Niagara Falls. We crossed Rainbow Bridge on foot to enjoy the view and have a picnic lunch. In the little park above the falls, while Mom prepared our lunch, David and I sat on some rocks at the edge of the falls, dangling our feet in the fast-flowing water as we held onto a railing. A strange cracking sound over and above the noise of the falls drew our attention. We turned around to see a large crack forming and expanding rapidly. Soon the fire department arrived and ushered everyone away from the edge of the cliffs and told us to leave the park. We came back to the Canadian side and watched in amazement as the rocks and railing where we had been sitting breakaway and fall dramatically to the river below.

In late August of that year, we took a trip to the Canadian National Exhibition (CNE), which had been an annual event since 1879. We had heard of the fun and games there, and we're excited to join in. As we neared the main gates, Dad said that the traffic was unusually heavy and there was a large crowd of people flocking towards the beach. Anxious to know what the excitement was, Dad parked the car and we joined the throng, arriving at the same time amid cheers to see Marilyn Bell, a sixteen-year-old girl, just complete her swim across Lake Ontario—the first to achieve that feat.

The company Dad worked for, Werner's Aluminum, held a family picnic for their employees and families. We went to the Brock's Monument, which is in Queenstown Heights on the Niagara parkway. The beautiful park commemorates the War of 1812. We learned a little history and got to climb inside the monument on the broken, narrow stairway, which brought us to an awe-inspiring view of the Niagara River. We also got our very first taste of watermelon, which we thought tasted like sweet water. What a large strange fruit! What would they think of next?

One exceptional trip was to Canada's capital, Ottawa. Dad rented a little housekeeping cottage on the Ottawa River, and we took a number of tours throughout the city. The agricultural building had a bull that was, I think, the largest in Canada. It was bigger by far than our car. We also had privy to the passing of a bill in parliament regarding Canada's fishing rights to the Grand Banks of Newfoundland. It was very interesting and amazing to discover the amount of yelling and arguing that occurs when the politicians are voting. Very surprising that parliament can ever accomplish anything!

On a second trip to the States, we headed for the Maine Coast. Dad had rented a little housekeeping cabin just a block from the ocean. There were miles of beautiful beaches, and frequently, docks with little shacks jutted out from the sandy shore. Many of those huts were actually cafés serving lobster caught right off the end of the dock. While we had lunch at one of those cafés, the chef motioned David and me to the kitchen. On the stove was a huge cauldron of boiling water, and a counter top had a number of live lobsters wandering aimlessly around. The chef picked up a lobster and deftly dropped it into the boiling water. We heard a screeching noise and inquired what it was. He responded, "You'd scream two if I drop you into boiling water." I have never eaten lobster since!

September had arrived with the anticipation of starting a new school in the country. The school was a one-room, one-teacher building, with a well and a bathroom (outside) situated on a lonely one-car width dirt road, known today as Taunton Road. From the main Highway 12, three farms stretched the entire length of the road. Dad had shown us where the school was so that we knew where to go. About two miles from home, we could either walk up the highway or take the "shortcut" to school, cutting through the sand pit, forest, and farmer's field. Mom said she was too busy with our sister to take us to our first day of school, and Dad had left to work; she told us to inform the teacher that she would sign any papers after the first semester.

The classroom had a total of twenty-seven students (grades 1 to 8). We were seated with two other students for what we thought was that total Grade 5 class. At the end of our first semester at Christmas, we found out we were actually back in Grade 4 again and the same age as the other two students. No wonder the teacher thought we were so smart!

The country school, known as Sinclair's School, turned out to be a lot of fun. On hot days, the classes were moved outside where we could catch a breeze under the trees. On cooler days, we learned square dancing, and on cold days, we could bring our skates and make use of the large pond that was across the road (now a cemetery!). Everyone always brought a packed lunch because everyone lived too far away, mostly at local farms. Therefore, our lunch hour gave us more time and opportunity to play. At harvest time in the fall, only a few children attended school, as most had to help bring in the hay and other farm duties.

During our school's field day competition, since there were not enough children of similar ages to compete, we alternated field day with another country school two miles west of Highway 12 so we would have enough competitors.

When I found out that my eyesight wasn't up to par, Mom and Dad took me to the optometrist, Neil Murkar, in Whitby. His office was at the "four corners" upstairs, and he fitted me with my first pair of glasses for short sightedness. I almost fell down the stairs when leaving because I wasn't used to seeing so well and I felt off balance. A week later, I was back because I had broken my glasses. A week after that, I repeated the trip. Dr. Murkar asked me what I was doing to keep breaking my glasses. "Well," I said, "I am the dodge ball champion at school, and the boys always aim at me first and my glasses keep getting hit by the ball." I was told not to wear then unless I need to see the blackboard better. The case of the broken glasses solved!

Of **Pitfalls** and **Pratfalls**

At the end of our Grade 7 year, a fire gutted our school. It was started by embers from the potbellied stove in the middle of the classroom. Every day until our school was rebuilt, we had to walk to school to catch a bus to be transferred to Brooklin, a few miles away north. That school year was horrible, as the Brooklin children taunted us and bullied the younger kids because we were "country hicks." We were thankful to leave that school and return to our newly renovated school when Grade 8 began. There were now more students, and as the area continued to grow, the school expected higher enrollment, so they had added more classrooms. There were still only four of us in Grade 8 at that time, and the room echoed whenever anyone talked.

In October, we got an abrupt introduction to Canada's unpredictable weather. Hurricane Hazel, a Category 4 hurricane, blew into our lives. Our roof blew away, and the neighbours across our street decided everyone would be safer in their newly built house. All the adults in the street met at each house and transfer each child, person to person, to the safety across the street. The wind was so strong we would have been blown away. For hours, everyone remained huddled together on the floor of the house while the house shook and the winds deafened us. When the storm died down, we went outside to survey the damage.

Winter in the country is an experience to love or hate. Our first winter in Toronto was slushy, dirty, and cold. But in the country, everything was white and fluffy. We could build snowmen and angels. Shovelling was a drag but easier to build snow forts in the piled-up snow. There was a large hill across the road behind my friend Brenda's house. It was actually a sand pit with relatively steep sides. It was an ideal toboggan hill once covered in snow. We could glide downwards, then sailed over the drop-off to land in a deep snowbank. Once, after coming down on a sled, I was making the climb back up the drop off as David was coming down in the toboggan. As my head peered over the hill, he ran over my face! When I went home, my mother said that nothing could be done for a broken nose because they couldn't put a cast on a nose.

Brenda

Brenda's dad was a well-known architect and originally designed their large ranch house to be a dance hall, but in the 1950s, it was unpractical because very few young people had cars and the hall was not well located. The family turned the building into their home, and I spent many nights and days there. Brenda's brother and sister were considerably older, with families of their own, so she was frequently left alone if her parents wanted to go out. I became her "companion" on those days to keep her company.

One winter, there were some workmen cleaning out the septic tank in Brenda's backyard. We were playing in the snow when her mother called us to come in from the bitter cold and get a hot chocolate. At the same time, a sudden blizzard hit and we ran for cover. As we raced for the backdoor, Brenda yelled, "Lookout for the—" But it was too late; I fell through the snow and ice layer on top of the septic tank. Unfortunately, it had not been emptied yet and I was up to my neck in sewage. Everyone frantically pulled me out, and I had to strip out of my snowsuit outside while a large bath towel was wrapped around me. I was carried inside to a large bathtub, and my entire wardrobe, including boots, was sent to the incinerator. I believe I truly earned the extra mug of hot chocolate.

My mother often referred to me as an "accident waiting to happen," but I can't claim to be alone in that. David had his own ups and downs. In summer, we could sometimes get enough kids gathered to have a game of baseball in the sand pit next to our street. The younger kids were only too happy to chase after the balls in the outfield. That left about four or five of us to actually play. The rule was whoever gets over the fence and to first base first was up to bat. Although I swear he got a head start, David hopped over the fence and landed in the middle of a hornet's nest. I am sure he would've won a gold medal in the Olympics for his run that day. He managed to run home and was sitting on the couch with Mom pulling out stingers from his legs and feet (right through his Keds) before the rest of us even got there.

David and I had a paper route for two different publishers. The *Toronto Telegram* bundles were dropped off around two p.m., and the local *Oshawa Times* at six p.m. We would deliver at both times to all the houses in our neighbourhood and again, later, twice to one house a mile north on Highway 12 and then to a house a mile south. Collecting was a nightmare, as in the country, we had to try to find people who lived far distances and with very long driveways. At that time, it wasn't acceptable dropping the paper at the end of a driveway, but on the bright side, we received a lot of nice gifts at Christmas from our customers, and every year, the *Oshawa Times* held a special party with a movie, hot dogs, candy, and lots of prizes to show their appreciation.

When we were younger during the summer holidays, when Dad had his vacation, we would see a little more of the country. One year we went across Canada and the United States to Yellowstone Park on a camping trip. The campsites were large areas with lovely bathrooms, showers, and laundry facilities. The garbage cans were buried in the ground with screwed-on lids to discourage wandering bears.

One night, after our tent was setup, we went to the bathroom to prepare for bed while Mom stayed behind to get our bedding ready. Suddenly we heard a blood curdling scream from the camping area. Everyone, including the park rangers, ran to see what was happening. Mom had heard someone trying to get into the tent, so, thinking it was us, opened the tent flaps and came nose to nose with a large black bear. I'm not sure which one ran the fastest—the bear or Mom? That was our last night camping.

Banff National Park

Going north, we visited beautiful national parks, like Banff and Glacier National Park, and stayed in motels for the rest of the trip. We arrived in Calgary, Alberta, during the time of the famous stampede. Lots of real-life cowboys and Indigenous peoples with impressive costumes. The traffic was halted for a parade, so Dad parked the car. We were just in time to see her Royal Highness Princess Margaret drive past. Luckily, Dad had his camera. Strange that we had to come to Canada to see British royalty!

We then travelled north to Edmonton and visited an aunt of Mom's. I hadn't been aware that we had relatives other than Uncle David and Aunt Helen in Toronto. It turned out that some of Dad's family had immigrated to the United States, Texas in particular. My granny had a brother that had immigrated to the U.S. He was the Hanna of Hanna Barbera, cartoon producers. But we never travelled south to Texas. We travelled east to come back home. Saskatchewan ended up being miles and miles of flatland, dotted occasionally by silos. The weather was extremely hot. Obviously, cars didn't have air conditioning in the early fifties, so the ride was uncomfortable. Dad stopped on the side of the highway at one point and took a photo of a rock, as it was the only thing of interest. Manitoba was a washout really! It rained the entire time we drove through, and Winnipeg was only observed to have miles of factories and nothing else of interest. Northern Ontario was dotted with mines and an amazing number of reserves.

Throughout our earlier years, we accumulated a variety of pets: Neko, the cat; Bimbo, the dog; assorted rabbits; and then my very own little turtle that I affectionately named Myrtle. Myrtle survived a little over a year before she died from a soft shell. Naturally, a small funeral service followed. We had acquired a little bantam hen, and Dad and David built a lovely henhouse in the back garden. It had an ordinary door for entering the interior, and a small door at ground level, opening into a little courtyard surrounded by a tall mesh fence to discourage any foxes. A rooster followed to keep the bantam company. Every day, David would collect the tiny eggs, and if there was enough on the weekend, we would enjoy scrambled eggs. The eggs were the size of a grape. David's job was feeding the birds and keeping their abode clean and warm. One very cold winter day, he forgot to close their little courtyard door and we found the rooster had frozen to death, though the little bantam (female) survived to live another day.

We had two little goldfish in a bowl in the dining room. One evening, Mom and Dad arrived home after a very late party. Mom was quite "jolly"; she took off her shoes and manage to weave up to her bed. In the morning, our little goldfish were missing from their bowl. Occasionally, they were known to jump out of the water, so we started searching the floor. Mom came downstairs, a little under the weather and still partially dressed, when we found our goldfish. They were squished onto the bottom of her stocking feet. The poor goldfish (what we could scrape up) were given the appropriate funeral. It really had only been a matter of time before they would have met their ultimate demise. A few weeks before their untimely deaths, Mom was changing the water in their bowl at the kitchen sink when the fish decided to escape. Mom turned on the tap, and they made a dash for it and promptly went down the drain. She quickly turned off the tap and yelled for Dad. He went outside where a slab of cement covered the septic tank just under the kitchen window. He lifted the cement, held the bucket under the drain from the kitchen, told Mom to turn on the tap, and the two escapees dove into the bucket, unharmed.

Throughout the centuries, inventions have improved the lives of millions. One such invention improved my life. I remember the day that the floor polisher salesman knocked at the door. At our house, we, or should say David and I, had daily chores. David was responsible for lawn mowing, snow shovelling, hedge trimming, daily shoe polishing, and pet feeding. My job was washing and drying dishes, setting the tables for meals, bed making, laundry on Mondays during the summer holidays, dusting, and removing scuff marks from the hardwood floors in the dining room, living room, and hallway and applying a layer of floor wax. After the wax was dry, I would polish the floors by hand. You can imagine my delight when the salesman demonstrated the newfangled floor polisher. The gadget not only cleaned but applied wax and polished floors in no time at all. I am not known for praying, but that day Mom bought that miraculous floor polisher, I made an exception—hallelujah!

Immediately across the street from our house was a restaurant. Because we lived on Highway 12, it was a relatively busy place to stop for coffee or a sandwich for people on the way north to the cottage country. The highway was the only main road north at the time. A young family with a newborn baby bought the business, and I got my first non-babysitting job there. The lady's husband worked daily in town, so his wife managed the restaurant. She spent most of the time in the back of the building where their living quarters were while I served the customers. One particularly hot day, a couple of tourists stopped by for a coffee. The lady was wearing a fur coat and was obviously uncomfortable with the heat. They said they were from the States and wanted to go skiing in Canada. They were very surprised at the hot weather and wondered where the ski hills were and how the snow could exist at those temperatures. I explained that only water skiing was possible until the wintertime. They were genuinely surprised and said they might as well go back home to Buffalo!

In 1954, we were introduced to a new tradition: Sadie Hawkins Day, which was held only on February 29, a leap year. I believe it was made popular due to a comic strip *L'il Abner*. The idea was that every four years, on that day, girls were allowed to ask a boy out on a date. Our school decided to celebrate the occasion by having all the girls make a lunch box decorated with flowers and hearts, and they would be auctioned off to the boys. The boys would get to enjoy a homemade lunch with the girl who provided the box. The boxes were to be anonymous so that no one would know whom they were sharing a lunch with.

I liked a particular boy named Lloyd and wanted him to bid for my box, which contained fried chicken, salad, cake, and a soda. Unfortunately, our neighbour's two younger brothers were visiting and temporarily attending our school. The one named Dennis (we called him "Dennis the Menace") was a pest. He constantly followed me around making rude remarks, and I'd totally disliked him. I even saw him eating dog food from a can to show off. Yuck! He bribed David to tell him which box was mine. Most bids for the boxes were sold for ten cents to twenty-five cents. Lloyd and Dennis both bid on my box. When the price got to three dollars, the teacher halted the biding and Dennis had lunch with me. What angered me was that he didn't like fried chicken, didn't eat salads, and the cake wasn't his preferred flavour. I told him that if I had known he was going to get my box, I would have just substituted the lunch for dog food because that was what he deserved.

Around that time, David had a serious incident with our beloved dog, Bimbo, the beagle. He was walking him on a leash, mainly to discourage him from bringing home more rabbits from the fields, and we were gathering all the neighbourhood kids to determine if a baseball game could be achieved when a very large dog, likely part Great Dane, ran towards us in attack mode. The dog belonged to the previous owners of the restaurant and was well known to go after several neighbourhood cats and had killed two. It was known to be vicious and always ran loose.

Due to this threat, David often carried a bow and arrows for protection. When the monster attacked Bimbo that day, ripping a chunk of the flesh and skin from his backside, David took aim with his bow and managed to hit the dog in the upper front leg. The arrow bounced off and the dog turned tail and ran home. We took Bimbo to the vet and he managed to recover. The owners of the dog called the police and claimed the dog was shot with an arrow and had pulled it out with its teeth. They said the dog was a very valuable show dog, winning of many ribbons. They threatened to sue us for a large sum of money. Mom phoned a lawyer, and the police interviewed all of us as witnesses. They also investigated the restaurant owners and found the dog had a bad reputation, and the entire street was fearful of the vicious animal. The fraudsters weren't able to extort money from us and were warned that they could be charged with giving false evidence, having no control of a dangerous animal, and a slew of other charges. The restaurant closed shortly after the incident, and the owners plus dog moved away to parts unknown.

Occasionally there were downsides to living in the country. It didn't help that we lived close to a sand pit. One particularly warm summer, there was an unbelievable surge of sand fleas. Poor Bimbo and Neko were beside themselves with a constant onslaught. Mom sent me to the basement one day to fetch something, and I was astonished to see the floor moving. The flea situation was rampant and we ended up flooding the basement and using the sump pump to get rid of the scourge. We did go through a great many bottles of calamine lotion that summer.

The basement was usually an interesting place, divided into different areas. Dad had a small space where he would repair our shoes when needed and kept his tools there as well. There was an area for coal just below a window and that held a coal chute; we used it to fuel our furnace in the winter. There was also play area where David kept his large comic book collection. That, of course, was completely destroyed by the flood due to the flea infestation.

One year, the LCBO employees went on a very lengthy strike. When the neighbourhood bootlegger ran out of beer and liquor, Mom and Dad decided to make their own beer. They used large rain barrels from outside, bought a bottling kit, and prepared their brew. Hops in potato bags and large tins of liquid malt were used for the process. The hops smelled terrible, but I had an addiction to the delicious malt. Every day, I would go downstairs with a large spoon and "taste test" the malt. The tin was large, and I reasoned that no one would notice a few spoonful's missing. Unfortunately, I didn't realize that a full tin was required in their brew, and I had left the tin barely half full. My reasoning that the mice probably got into the tin fell on deaf ears!

Beyond the forest and sand pits across the road was a lovely creek below what became Cochrane Street. We decided to spend a day fishing, but Mom was going to be busy, so we had to take Diana with us. We found her constant whining and complaining very annoying, and it was difficult to keep her quiet. There frequently was a group of young thugs that often came north from Whitby to harass the "country hicks." They carried rifles and would often shoot at us. A few of us had built a number of forts hidden in the underbrush of the forest where we could hide and lay undetected until the juveniles passed by. We constantly told Diana to be quiet so we wouldn't attract attention as we resumed our fishing. David flipped his fishing pole with hook and worm when he accidentally caught Diana in the back with the hook. She started screaming while we tried to unhook her and, obviously, brought attention to our location. Luckily, the intruders included a girl my age, called Linda, and her older brother, Graham, who lived between the creek and Cochrane Street. They accompanied us to their house where Diana was released from the hook. Linda remained a good friend for many years after.

David and Bob

The creek was always a fun place. We would ice skate on it in the winter and fish and swim in the summer. We learned about some deeper water areas for swimming and, after shooing cows away, would have the swimming holes to ourselves. One day, we were visited by some health officials at our door. They inquired about any illnesses in the household. Apparently Brenda's nephew, who was the same age as her, had come down with typhoid fever. Randy usually came swimming with us and had been told a number of times not to drink the water, but he had not paid attention and was lucky to recover from the dreaded disease. Lesson learned!

Country life seems to invite unusual accidents. One summer day, David and his friend Bob Campbell were sitting in the backyard deep in conversation. Bob lived half mile down Highway 12, and he and David were in the Air Cadets together. They remained best friends for many years. Anyway, being nosy, I decided to creep behind the garage and listen in on their conversation. They heard me, so I turn to run away and accidentally ran onto a railway spike attached to a piece of wood. The spike went through my shoe and up into my leg via my heel. I was absolutely speechless, and David and Bob carried me into the house. Mom cut the shoe off and pulled the spike out while my brother and friend wailed loudly. I couldn't say anything until Mom stuck my foot into a sink full of Dettol. Then I joined in the wailing. When Dad got home for dinner, he took me to the doctor's office in town to receive a tetanus shot. Luckily, the spike didn't break any bones. It had gone straight in and just missed my ankle bone by a fraction.

My First exhibited painting

I had always enjoyed painting (usually landscapes) from an early age after receiving brushes and oil paints one Christmas. An elderly lady living down the road from us told Mom she also liked to paint and belonged to an art club in Brooklin. She convinced my parents that I could attend the club once a week. The Brooklin Art Guild was mentored by a well-known artist, Ray Hall, and consisted mostly of retired men and women. They welcomed me and encourage my artistic skills. After a year, they held an art show for the community and I got to exhibit one of my completed paintings. I was thirteen years old at the time, and apparently, it was unusual for someone my age to contribute to a show. Photographers from Toronto and local newspapers came to our house to take pictures of my painting.

My friends Brenda's father was an accomplished architect and artist. He was the head designer for Sklar furniture and built a large showroom in front of his house to exhibit furniture for Sklar. He had a disagreement with his company, so he quit his job and returned to his very successful career designing hotels and elaborate homes. The showroom was turned into an art gallery. I spent a lot of time at the family home, keeping Brenda company while her parents were away. Her father was interested in my artwork and started exhibiting my paintings after framing them in his gallery. A lot of my work was purchased by the owners of the hotels that he had designed, and I earned a considerable amount of money, sometimes selling five or more paintings a month. I also designed and made samples of a variety of different aprons for the waitresses at a motel and restaurant called the Sun Dial in Orillia.

When David and I were in Grade 8, Diana started school in Grade 1. Mom and Dad decided that the school was too far for her to walk, so they hired a taxi to take us and a few other of the kids from the street at a shared cost to and from the school. The taxi was very large with glass behind the driver, who was elderly and quite deaf. There were little seats actually on the back door panel. David always sat on the door seat. One day, driving home, it seemed the backdoor wasn't closed properly, and while going over the bumpy dirt road, the door opened and the seats and David went flying out of the car. He managed to grab the door handle and hung on running beside the car. Everyone was yelling for the driver to stop, but he couldn't hear us. We pounded on the glass, jumped up and down, and actually shook the whole car before he finally stopped. Luckily, David was shaken but not hurt, although his shoes had seen better days. My parents insisted that another driver drive us to school until the end of the school year.

Talk about accident prone—we came home from school one day to find fire trucks at our house. Apparently, Mom had been making French fries when the oil she was using spilled over the stove and set fire to the kitchen. She madly ran around the house, closing all the windows, dumped salt on the flames, and got the pan off the stove. The fire was put out, but the house, especially the kitchen, was completely covered in black soot. The fire department got all the smoke out, but it took weeks to wash the walls, windows, and all the dishes. Mom refused to talk about the fire or explain why she was cooking French fries in the middle of the afternoon. After all, she claimed she never ate anything but the occasional biscuit with her cup of tea.

When we became pre-teens, summers were more fun. Mom and Diana would leave us to go back home to Scotland. I was then in charge of the house. As well as usual duties, I did the shopping after making a weekly menu. I planned all the meals and cooked them, except Dad would often BBQ on weekends. He would give me the same weekly allowance that Mom got, drop me off of the grocery store, and pick me up a little later. I got to buy the products I liked, like my favourite cereal, meats, and vegetables.

On weekends, we took day trips. I would prepare picnic lunches, and we were off sightseeing or fishing. Dad always brought his camera and constantly snapped pictures of the countryside, David, and me. I think they were of us because he often cut off our heads in the picture. Near the end of summer vacation, we would drive to Montreal to pick up Mom and Diana, and then spend a week at a summer lodge or cabin.

One summer, Dad had rented a lone cabin on a tiny lake in Algonquin Park. It had a rowboat and a sandy beach. The lake was surrounded by forest, and the cabin so remote, we had to walk through thick foliage to reach it. The lake was so clear we could see the bottom, and the call of the loons woke David and me up early. We would then paddle out and enjoy the serenity and the wonder of the wild.

Because we had picked Mom and Diana up of the airport and didn't return home at that time, they had all their luggage at the cabin. One morning, we heard a lot of screaming from inside. Mom had been getting dressed and found a very expensive cashmere sweater set that she had bought in Glasgow full of holes. Apparently the chipmunks had found her sweaters, which they thought were very suitable for nesting and comfortable bedding, and helped themselves.

On the bright side, they had been kind enough to leave a considerable number of nuts as a replacement. There is honour even with the smallest of thieves!

After the summer holiday, we entered Grade 9 at Whitby District High School, later changed to Henry Street High. We travelled daily by school bus, but because I had joined a number of extracurricular clubs (which surprisingly became part of the regular curriculum in later years), I often found that I had to walk home along the highway.

High school took some getting used to: we had larger classrooms, some with thirty-eight students each, different classrooms, and different teachers for each subject. We seemed to spend a lot of time walking the halls, looking for the next class. Students were required to supply all their own textbooks, binders, paper, pencils, and pens for each subject. Because of the costs, most students took summer jobs. A lot of my schoolmates worked at the canning factory in Whitby or picked fruit and vegetables. I did a lot of babysitting, and some parents hired me for a few hours to entertain their children with stories that I'd made up. It surprised me when some of the adults stayed home with their kids because they found my stories of "The "Little Lost Leaf" and "The Little Sausage" and some other such children's nonsense amusing. But I did manage to make enough to pay for all my school supplies.

Because I was getting older, I was assigned more responsibility for Diana. On Halloween, she was going to a party at a church in Whitby for children that joined their drop-in play-time group. I was given the task of dressing Diana in a Halloween costume. I used some bright red stretchy pajamas to make a hood and made black paper horns and a long black tail with a triangle on the end. A trident finished the costume. Mom was horrified and said she couldn't go to a church party dressed as a devil. I started all over again, thinking a pregnant nun wouldn't go over well either, so I pulled out all my net and lace crinolines and dressed her as a bride. When she came home after the party, she was very angry because the kid that won the "best costume" award was dressed in a paper devil costume.

In high school, my pet peeve was my foot attire. All my friends and schoolmates wore "white bucks" or "saddle shoes." My mother decided that only dumpy brown Oxfords were practical and lasted longer. I constantly complained, to no avail, that they hurt my feet. One day, Dad had taken the shoes downstairs to his workshop to re-heel them (they lasted longer) and discovered that a tack had penetrated through to the inside, explaining why my feet hurt. I had ended up with a hard painful callous on my heel. I eventually grew out of those shoes and Mom bought me a pair of plastic sandals. I broke out in an extremely annoying rash and itch. Mom said it was athlete's foot and bought cream to cure it, saying I should be back in Oxfords. One day, our doctor was visiting (Mom and Dad played bridge with him and his wife) and he noticed my constant scratching at my feet. He took a look and said it wasn't athlete's foot at all but an allergy to the plastic sandals and the cream had made it worse. I was able to graduate to canvas tennis shoes.

When we turned sixteen, David and I had our first birthday party. As we were still living in the country, we were only able to invite the local kids and school chums that were in walking distance to help us celebrate. We had the usual: hot dogs, Lipton chicken noodle soup, cake, and ice cream—a fare that became a tradition for my own children many years later before families felt obligated to entertain their offspring and guests at restaurants and entertainment venues. We, however, were content to square dancing and playing word games

Looking back many years, I am totally surprised that David and I actually survived our years in the country. I remember well the times we went swimming at Springhill Park, just a few miles off Highway 12. The large pool was filled with creek water; there was no lifeguard, but a rope stretched over the pool to indicate the deep end versus the shallow. A few of us enjoyed playing in the pool, and David and his friend Bob liked to duck my girlfriend and me under water. One time, after being ducked, I came up under the rope underwater and couldn't surface. My mother's friend realized I was at the bottom of the pool and dove in to bring me up. It took a few minutes of artificial respirations before I could vomit and breathe again. A few weeks later, the family took a trip to Lake Simcoe. A small sandy beach and sandbars extended out into the lake. Between each sandbar, the water got increasingly deeper. Mom put her arm around my waist when I could no longer reach bottom. Unfortunately, she tripped and went underwater, completely forgetting she was still holding me. I ended up side down before she realized I was drowning. Back to resuscitation time! I also didn't fare too well in the winter. I already had a broken nose when David ran over my face with the toboggan, so when I decided to fly down a snowy hill on a metal saucer, it was completely my fault. The saucer hit a rock, leaving a big dent in the centre of the saucer and me with a broken tail bone. Walking home was very painful, but you can't put a cast on a bottom!

Chapter 5

We Are Growing Up

Part 1: School

When we entered Grade 10, we moved into the town of Whitby into a custom-built house, only a block from the school on Burns Street. I continued babysitting at the homes of my parents' friends and at various cottages in the summer. I started getting an allowance of twenty dollars a month to buy my clothes, school supplies, cosmetics, personal items, and entertainment. Of course, I was expected to continue with my household duties. Mom was delighted to have a maid again, but she only came one day a week because she shared her with a friend.

The day before the maid came, I had double duty, like extra cleaning in the bathrooms and kitchen, because Mom didn't want the maid to tell her friends that she kept a dirty house. David had his usual duties, like shoe polishing, lawn cutting, snow shoveling, and so on. During the summer, we no longer went on family vacations. Mom and Diana often went back to Scotland, and when Dad had his vacation weeks, my parents and Diana would go on holiday. We weren't always privy to where they were going.

School classes, homework, and after school clubs kept me exceedingly busy. The art club gave me the ability to express my artistic talents. One year, our club spent many months making masks for Whitby's yearly anniversary parade. We used large cardboard boxes, stove or washing machines size, and decorated them to look like faces. We applied giant ears, noses, and eyes. A variety of objects, like straw and wool, contributed to arms, hair, and colorful clothes. They were suitable to climb inside to entertain the crowds at the parade. Unfortunately, our hard work was for naught, as a rain storm dampened the festivities and we were cancelled due to the imminent destruction of our heads.

For most of my high school years, I designed the school yearbook, "the Hi Lite," and went to the school office during quiet class time to stencil my designs. I was also in charge of decorating the gymnasium for a variety of functions, like dances, the prom, and school plays, and put up dozens of posters advertising a large variety of events.

When I graduated from Grade 12, the club stopped running, and instead, art had been introduced into the curriculum and became a subject for Grade 9 students. The student with the highest marks was even awarded a prize, much like the students who excelled in math and the sciences. However, when I attended graduation, after the end of the school year, along with my diploma, I was surprised to be presented with a special gift for the years of work I had put in for my artistic contribution. I was quite embarrassed but deeply honored. Unlike the plaques the other recipients got, I received a top-of-the-line purse in a gigantic box.

I was also a member of the badminton club, and our team won standing in the Ontario school competition. I had fun with the archery club too. We used large bull's eye targets at the back of the school and long bows, which required more ability than crossbows. In spite of only having a thirty-four-pound pull, I manage to hold my own in competition with my teammates. When I went into Grade 12, it became permissible for girls to join the curling club. David was a member of the team, so I was happy to join in. We formed our own teams with David as skip, me as second, my friend Kathy McIntyre as lead, and David's friend Herb Gray as vice. We ended up as league champs and awarded the large trophy with our names engraved on it. We were allowed to exhibit the trophy in our homes for three months. We retained it for six months, and the trophy is still on display under glass in the school to this day, as far as I know.

WIN STUDENT CURLERS TROPHY

For the past few years our ... ... Pictured above wi... right are Bill Moreat, Kathy ... were league champs in a ... of Henry Street High ... Bill Mowat is the winni... McIntyre, lead, Dorothy Jack ... ... high school curling ... had been actively on... high school rink who won...

One year I was voted into the school student council, which turned out to be very interesting, to say the least. We reviewed and attempted to resolve problems with the students and school itself. We offered opinions regarding school uniforms versus dress codes and even in changing of the name of the school when the building of another high school on Anderson Street had begun. But as with typical politics, we found out how irrelevant our voices were when Durham District School Board vetoed all our decisions—proving to us that the opinions of the little people don't count.

Everyone has their favourite school subjects. I really enjoyed English literature and ancient history but had trouble with the math, although algebra was okay. Luckily, David excelled at math and helped me with my homework. One year, during modern history (which I found exceedingly boring), we were given a project to write an essay on a specific form of government. I chose communism and thought I was being innovative by writing to the Russian embassy, asking for information about their politics and its effects and benefits to the population. I received a reply from the embassy, which included a large package of pamphlets and propaganda. A few days later, Mom was annoyed when I got home from school because the RCMP had shown up at our door demanding to see me. Apparently, they spy on embassy mail and, because of the Cold War at this time, were under the impression I was a communist and was prepared to arrest or possibly deport me. My mother went up one side of these officers and down the other, calling them a few choice names, as they were targeting a child simply doing a school project. They slinked away, hopefully feeling as stupid as they looked.

As an award for passing Grade 12 (he went on to Grade 13), David got my parents to co-sign for a '52 Morris Minor car. When we were going to the curling club on Brock Street North, he would drive everyone in his little car so we all didn't have to walk through the snow and cold. There were frequently a lot of us, and so we didn't quite fit into the small space; instead, many of us hung out the doors holding on for dear life. David always enjoyed driving into very large snow banks at the side of the road too. Everyone would have to pile out, pick up the car, and repeat the procedure all over again until we got to our destination.

Home economics was always an enjoyable class for me. Half of the school year was sewing for girls and metalworking for boys. One teacher we had for sewing was an older (much older) lady, who bragged about never having to purchase any wearable items, including her undergarments. She pulled up her dress to show us her long bloomers, which almost reached to her knees, and told us that all proper young ladies should be wearing this type of undergarment. Her camisole was around the same vintage. I think she was truly unaware that this was the generation of miniskirts and skorts.

One time, we were attempting to learn how to properly attach a puff sleeve to a bodice. My friend was getting more and more frustrated because she couldn't master it. Finally with much aplomb, she yelled, "I got it." She had finally managed to sew her long sleeve to the rest of the blouse and held it up in triumph. However, the cuff was now attached to the middle of her blouse. This was one of the funniest things I'd seen in a while and couldn't stop laughing. The rest of the class follow suit and burst out laughing also. The face of our prim and proper teacher turned red in frustration at our hysterics, and for the first time in my life, I was sent to the principal's office. I laughed all the way down the hall at the absurdity of the situation and told the office staff what happened. The principal told me to return to class and try to keep a straight face, and he joined his staff, who were hiding fits of laughter.

Cooking class was highly enjoyable. Mrs. McIntyre was a jolly pleasant woman and taught me cooking throughout my high school years. She lived in an old beautiful century home with her husband (a highly respectable criminal lawyer), her son, Duncan Junior, and their daughter, Kathy, my curling inmate. Her house was elegantly decorated with many antiques. Due to the fact that her husband worked very long hours, I think she was lonely. Once a month, she would invite three or four girls from her cooking class to her home for a scrumptious dinner and conversation. I was always invited and look forward to socializing with such an interesting and intelligent woman.

Part 2: Dating

After school hours, a number of us would trot down to the Golden Gate, our favourite Chinese dining establishment, where we could play the table juke boxes and order a large plate of French fries with gravy and a number of forks depending on how many friends were present. My parents discouraged one-on-one "dates," so there were always a number of us at various outings.

The Anglican Church on Dundas Street held a teen dance in the basement on Friday nights, presumably to keep us out of trouble. My friend Patricia was a member of the church and a long time Girl Guide; it was her job to sit at the door and collect the small fee. I always sat as relief so she could dance and I assisted the DJ with the record selection and, occasionally, fill in as the DJ as well. At the end of the evening, the money collected was put into a cloth bag and then taken home to give to the church the following day. Patricia frequently went off with her boyfriend after the dance, so I took the bag of money, walking home by myself. I guess it was a different time because I never felt uncomfortable carrying all that money, and it never crossed my mind that I could easily be robbed.

On Saturdays, my friend Linda Borchuk and I would go to the arena on Brock Street South to skate. Afterwards, we would go upstairs to a teen club where we could sit with a Coke and socialize to the sound of music. This was a typical evening until some "punks" on motorcycles from Ajax disrupted our good time. They brought beer (drinking age was 21) and picked fights with everyone. Their disrupted and disrespectful behaviour caused our after-skating fun to come to an end after three or four weeks of this.

One Easter, before going skating, Linda wanted to go to church for the special service; she was a Catholic. We left our skates at the main entrance, and she went to the front of the very crowded church, while I sat at the back where she told me no one would notice me. I felt very uncomfortable, so I took a seat in an empty pew. A lot of parishioners kept turning to look at me, and I wondered how they knew I wasn't Catholic. Just before the service started, a priest walked all the way from the front of the church, came directly to where I was sitting, bent down to whisper in my ear, and asked me if I was going to take up the collection for the evening because I was sitting in the "usher's pew." I decided it would be safer if I'd just got my skates and waited outside for Linda!

My parents decided that I could date during the weekends. Curfew was 11:30 and going steady was forbidden. They insisted on meeting my dates at the door. Actually, Mom was the one who wanted to check each boy out and find out their family history. I learned to "train" my suitors to act excessively polite and to complement my mother. It worked like a charm. One particular "boyfriend" whom I found to be a bully and nasty to some of my male friends was able to charm my mother. She decided I should continue to date him. His family was well-to-do, and therefore, he was a good match. One Halloween, she got me out of the bath to go out with that "nice" Russell when he showed up late at the door. I gave him a piece of my mind and dumped him. About four years later, after my mother and I ran into him, she asked me or rather told me that I should be dating that "nice" boy. I never heard another word from her when I told her that he had just gotten out of the Kingston penitentiary for rape and attempted murder. Certainly not, as she thought, the "right kind" of boy!

David was comfortable hanging out with our group, which told me that he thought it was time to actually date a girl. Soon enough, he asked me for advice on how to behave and what was expected. He was very taken with my girlfriend Linda, so I instructed him to phone her with an invitation to dinner or a movie. Then I told him to give a definite time when he'd pick her up in his car, to not honk the horn but go to her door, and to open the car door for her. I also told him that he should pay for the meal and anything else, and just make small talk. He took it all in and practised with me until I gave him my approval. After he had his "date," Linda told me about their evening. Apparently, his attempt at "small talk" in the car was in looking longingly at her and saying, "Do you shave your eyebrows?" We laughed for quite a while, and I gave him another lesson on what to talk about. He settled on: "You look very lovely to night." Lesson learned!

Drive-in movies was a big thing in the fifties and sixties. Two movies, a newsreel, a cartoon, and popcorn or hot dogs from the concession were great when snuggling in the comfort of the car. My problem was my curfew of 11:30, which meant I would always miss the second movie.

The annual prom was held on a yearly basis and was only for the Grade 12 graduates and a partner. I was looking forward to the festivities, which were held in the school gym. I had a date (a must) and our ticket. I was a little unsure of what to wear until my French teacher, Mrs. Phillips, who knew my parents, phoned me at home and asked me to visit. When I got to her house, just across from the school, she asked me if I had a prom dress yet. When I said that I was working on it, she brought out two beautiful gowns that had belonged to her daughter. She told me her daughter was now in university, no longer had any use for them, and would be pleased if I'd took them and enjoyed my night. I was beyond excited and thanked her profusely for the generous gift. Unfortunately, the day prior to my prom, Mom told me that a friend would not be able to curl with her the following day because her babysitter was ill and told me that a prom was only frivolous and I had to baby sit instead. I didn't even know the family whose children I was minding.

A week later, my friend Brenda called and said that her boyfriend's male friend hadn't asked anyone to his prom at OCVI in Oshawa because he was too shy. She begged me to be his blind date, and I thought since I already had a dress, why not. My date showed up in a brand-new Lincoln car to escort me to the dance. He was exceptionally pleasant and every inch a real gentleman. We had a good time and went to a fine restaurant afterwards, even though I got into trouble when I got home a little past curfew. I was called "rebellious" by Mom! Her friends that I baby sat for—the Roblins—told my mother that she was being totally unreasonable, so the subject of my "late night" was dropped.

The following new year, the Roblins asked me to come to Windsor with them to baby sit their children while they celebrated the new year with their close friends. I was told to bring a fancy dress, as some of the party was being held at their house. To my surprise, they had made arrangements for another baby sitter and I had a date made for the New Year. Dale was a charming man and had a responsible job in Detroit. He presented me with a beautiful orchid corsage, and we had a marvelous "my first new year's date" date. My mother was never told of her friends' betrayal, as they knew she never approved of anything I enjoyed. Dale continued to write to me for several months and called me a couple of times. When he sent a gorgeous bouquet of long stem red roses, my mother phoned him and told him to never contact me again. "Sending letters and flowers to a seventeen-year-old" was not appropriate in her eyes.

My parents enjoyed hosting a lot of parties and I was always required to attend. Mom said she needed help with serving snacks and cleanup. She really enjoyed games played in the dark as an excuse to take the opportunity to flirt with the male guests. One game that was a favourite was "sardines." One person was chosen to hide some where in the house "in the dark," and everyone else had to spread out to locate the first sardine. On finding him or her, they would quietly join them in the space until everyone was crammed into the area. Once I was the sardine and hid in a small two-piece bathroom in the corner of the basement. At the end of the game, there was over twelve people piled into the small space, and the toilet had to be taken apart to extricate me from behind where I had been lodged tightly after everyone crammed in.

Mom and Dad joined the local theatre group. They often produced one-act plays for local residents to enjoy. They managed to recruit me to help with background on the play *Blythe Spirit* by Noel Coward. It's a story of a woman who dies and returns as a ghost to create havoc on her husband who has taken up with another woman. He can see her most of the time, but no one else can. I was situated on the centre of the stage, crouched behind a sofa with a stack of small cushions. The play carried on for what seemed internal, and stiffness and cramps had set in when the "ghost" went on a rampage. Picture frames flew off the wall, furniture was overturned, and I threw the cushions from the back of the sofa in all directions. Because I couldn't see where I was throwing them, a number of theatre patrons were startled at the invisible projectiles coming out of nowhere.

Dad decided to take flying lessons at the Oshawa Airport. He eventually got his flying license, and Mom and Dad joined the flying club. They went on frequent flying breakfasts all over Canada and the USA and often took Diana and David up for short trips. When I eventually got a turn, I was amazed how flat everything looked from the air and the huge amount of green space around Oshawa and Whitby. Dad was a bit of a comedian, and that day, he cut the planes motor off. He pretended to panic, yelling for me to hang on. When I didn't react and told him to turn the engine on, I'd spoiled his joke. I don't scare easily and was well aware of his sense of humour.

Christine and Tommy

Mom's cousin Christine Wilson, nee Forgan, from Stirling, Scotland, moved to Canada with her infant son, Alain, to join her husband, Tommy, in 1954. Tommy was a professor of physics and chemistry, who had been recruited by Trinity College School (TCS) in Port Hope, a private boy's school for the elite. Coincidentally, Dad had actually attended school in Girvan, where they were both born and raised, so it was a great reunion. Most of the boys, many from Europe and Asian royalty, resided at the school, as did some of professors and their families. Tommy, Christine, and Alain had a lovely two-bedroom apartment in the school, and I was a frequent visitor. I would take a train from Oshawa to Port Hope, where Tommy would meet me, and often stayed the weekend and for weeks during the summer holidays. Tommy found it highly amusing when boys would approach him to ask permission to ask me out on a date—good manners were a must at the school.

The dining room was very large, with a head table where the professors eat and a small dining room adjacent to accommodate family members that occasionally enjoyed a ready-made meal. On one occasion, when a few people used the little dining room, we were invited to join the teachers at the head table. One lunch time, as I was putting Alain down for his nap, Christine said she would let everyone know I would be a little late and to start lunch without me. As it was raining outside, I was instructed to come in from the main hall, instead of where we usually enter the dining room. When I arrived, I was relieved to see everyone had started the meal; I figured I wouldn't be noticed making my way through the crowd of boys to the head table at the far end of the room. Unfortunately, I was noticed, and as etiquette demanded, every one of the boys—over two hundred and fifty!—stood up until I reached my seat. Christine and the professors were highly amused.

The school had its own swimming pool, tennis courts, and snack shop. I often spent enjoyable hours with a variety of activities with a number of dates. I was also invited to their annual prom, accompanied by the senior football champion. When Christine became pregnant again, they moved out of the school apartment into a beautiful century home, just outside of Port Hope, in the village of Welcome. Tommy became the headmaster of the school after a few years and deserved the prestigious appointment.

Part 3: Working for Fun and Profit

Nearing Christmas, I drew up a portfolio of a few Christmas designs, like you'd see on Christmas cards, and went around to all the downtown stores and businesses to see if they would like their front windows painted for the holidays. I used regular poster paint that could easily be washed off. I ended up with a lot of customers, some of which hired me to make up indoor posters and advertise sale events. The local corner pizza store had me write up their board menus as they changed. A bonus was a free pizza any day I wanted after the owner closed the shop in the evening. Rather than throwing the leftover pizza toppings out, he would pile them onto my pizza and hand deliver it before he went home. It was definitely the best pizza in town!

The pet store in the centre of Whitby asked me to paint their large front window to draw attention to the store. I painted large mermaids sitting on rocks. One very cold winter, I was mortified to learn there was a problem with the mermaids. The store itself was kept very warm, due to the large number of aquatic life and many small animals in the store, but the extreme cold outside caused a lot of condensation on the windows. The mermaids' breasts started to run, and I had to keep repairing them. It certainly brought a lot of attention to the store and was newsworthy enough to appear in the local newspaper.

David took a course on taxidermy and, one cold winter day, found a beautiful dead snowy owl at the side of a country road, apparently hit by a car. He brought it home and created an absolute masterpiece with the bird. Top marks!

He had a little workshop in his bedroom where he worked on his various projects. Just before Christmas, Mom asked me to bring something from the attic. Its entrance was located inside David's closet (we had a split-level house). There was no light, so I had to feel around for the box I had come for, and felt something very gooey on my hands. On inspection, I found out my hands were in a box filled with the decomposing innards of his owl. I think I used all the hot water taking a shower that day and ever after used a flashlight to retrieve anything from that attic.

One summer, I got a job at the local dairy bar. It was a small restaurant on the main street and was a truck stop for many travellers on their way to Montreal. At the time, Highway 401 had not been built yet and the police often steered the truckers to us. We served soups and stews in hearty servings, as well as a variety of ice cream cones and milkshakes. It was a busy little restaurant that also served the locals. An elderly gentleman who was a resident of Fairview lodge, the town's best well-kept long-term care home, would daily walk to our little restaurant. He always ordered a five-cent, one-scoop cone in the special flavour. We always had chocolate, vanilla, strawberry, and a special flavour, like walnut or butterscotch. He always insisted that I wait on him if I was working, and he always gave me a five-cent tip. Some of the nurses, who occasionally came to the restaurant, told me that the gentleman had always referred to me as his "girlfriend" to staff and other residents. One day, a nurse brought me an envelope that contained twenty-five cents. They said the elderly man had passed away; he wanted to make sure I got the money to remember my best customer and said he'd miss his girlfriend. A sad farewell!

I spent a month just about every summer in cottage country caring for children whose parents rented cottages. Usually, it was only the women and children that were there. Their husbands only came on weekends. There were also a lot of teenagers at each location doing the same job, and after the kids settled for the night, we had free time to attend a movie, perhaps in the town of Lindsay, go boating, play outdoor games, or fill the boat gas tanks and, on dark nights, go skinny dipping. One summer, the Roblins, who I baby sat for each summer, went to visit some friends on Jack Lake. Their friends' two teenage boys decided they would teach me to water ski. One of the boys would drive their boat, while the other kept a lookout. Flying off the dock, I was constantly thrown straight into the lake, so they tried starting me off on the Sandy Beach. Crouched down, I held tightly to the rope when the boat took off. It sped across the lake, leaving a giant wave. When the lookout couldn't see me, his brother sped up to try and locate where I'd come into the water. The problem was I didn't let go of the rope! When the boat left the beach, the rope caught between my legs and skinned my thighs. My mind kept telling me to hang on for dear life and I went around the lake still hanging on, underwater the whole way. After a lot of sputtering, calamine on my bleeding legs, the boys getting a lecture on safety, and an uncomfortable night, I resolved to never try water skiing again.

One of Dad's coworkers, who lived just north of us in the country, asked if I could baby sit for him. Mr. Hill was a very strange person. He also was in management, like Dad, and his wife, a quiet gentlewoman, was always extremely well dressed, her hair done professionally, and she had expensive jewelry and furs. Dad told me he was really "cheap" but that they wanted to leave the impression that they were well-to-do. They had a beautiful house, two small boys, and two dachshund dogs. The first time I went there, I entered the side door, which lead to the basement. The two little boys were watching TV and playing with toys scattered around the room. Their parents gave me instructions on how to care for their two dogs (they smelled horrible): when to watch them outside, where to fill their food bowls and water dishes, and where they went to bed with blankets. I asked about the children, and they said that the children knew how to do everything on their own. When the program they'd been watching ended, the two boys, who were about three and four, got up, turned off the TV, picked up all the toys and put them in a toy box, and quietly went upstairs. I ran their bath where they washed, wiped out the tub, put on pajamas, and quietly got into bed. I went downstairs to the kitchen to find a chain and a lock on the fridge door and all the cupboards locked as well. There was a glass of juice and a cookie on the counter, with a note that it was for me. I never heard a peep from the children all evening, and I checked on them every half hour, waiting for the penny to drop. But it was the dogs that were a pain: misbehaving and demanding, as well as stinky. When the family came home, Mr. Hill gave me the exact change, to the penny, after calculating the amount owed at forty-five cents an hour. When he left to start the car to take me home, his wife shook my hand to thank me and pressed a two-dollar bill into my palm, with a wink. I found out that each day, he would make a list of what and the amount each family member was to eat, take everything out of the fridge and cupboards to the exact amount for each, leave it on the counter, and relock everything up again until he got home. Dad said the management would take turns paying for lunch each day, usually to a nice restaurant. When Mr. Hill's turn was up, he would take everyone to a hot dog stand. Dad noted that when anyone else was paying, he ordered the most expensive items on the menu. I heard that a couple of years later, his wife filed for divorce. I was just surprised it wasn't sooner, and he got no support from his coworkers.

I had an interesting babysitting job just down at the lake in Whitby. There was a community of very luxurious homes on the beach. I stayed at one of them for a month. A doctor with three children and her husband, who already had three children, got married and had another child. I cared for their six children while the mother cared for the infant. The house was massive; the children, all around the same age, were all well behaved and enjoyed each other as friends and siblings. We spent many hours playing games, swimming in the lake, listening to stories, and walking on the beach. One day, the kids found a number of used condoms on the shore and asked me what they were. I quickly replied, "Oh! They're fish lungs." I let their mother know in case there was some confusion about condoms in the future.

While these homes were owned by the residents, the town of Whitby held a one-hundred-year lease on the land that the houses were on; when the leases expired, the houses were torn down for Hayden Shore Park, which the community used.

The Roblins lived in a little house in the middle of town. Their two children, Sally and Andrew, were very good children and always listened to me. The family's friends the Williams lived in Windsor but visited often, and every year, they shared a rented cottage. One fall day, before school started, they all decided to vacation for a week without the kids. The Williams children were the same age as the Roblins, but they also had a month-old baby. In spite of my mother's objections, especially with a baby, they insisted they had total faith and that I was extremely reliable. I had a list of activities, directions on making the formula for the infant, how to use their washer and dryer, and an emergency number that I hope we wouldn't need. I had no problems whatsoever, was paid well, and thoroughly enjoyed the experience.

The following year, the Roblins purchased a beautiful century home across from the high school. Every day, I would go to the house at lunchtime and make the children's lunches before we would all return to our respective schools. I then returned to the house after school, just as the kids got home. At that time, I would start them on their homework while I prepared snacks and started supper for the family when the parents got home from work. I frequently stayed overnight and was generally treated like a family member. Mrs. Roblin took me to the hairdresser's, bought me modern clothes, and my first pair of high heeled shoes, complete with a professional hostess to teach me how to walk properly in them. She was the swimming instructor at the Ontario Ladies College in Whitby, so I also got complete lessons on lifesaving techniques.

Chapter 6

Moving Forward

Part 1: David

David graduated from Grade 13 and entered teacher's college. He has always enjoyed teaching children and coaching children's soccer games and other sports. After finishing school, he was given a little country school to administer, something he could relate to from our early experience. He used to say that he was the principal, the vice principal, teacher, and janitor all in one. When most country schools closed down in Ontario, David resigned as a teacher and entered officer training for the military, following in our father's footsteps.

In 1965, he was a graduate and became a member of the very prestigious Black Watch regiment in Nova Scotia. After some years, he became a lieutenant and was sent to Cyprus, where an uprising had occurred. At home, we were aware of the many shootings and casualties, causing us as many days of anxiety. He wrote to me frequently to dispel my worry, saying his peace-keeping force was safe. Back at his home base, he wrote that Elizabeth The Queen Mother had visited (as the Black Watch was her regiment), along with another officer, and that they had enjoyed afternoon tea with the much loved and respected royal.

Lt. David Jack, son of Mr. and Mrs. Robert Jack, of Whitby, updates his records at Kanli Keny Dam outpost in Cyprus where he supervises the handling of construction material on behalf of the United Nations. Both Greek and Turk Cypriots are co-operating in construction at the site under UN supervision. Jack is a member of 1 Battalion, The Black Watch.

David in the national papers in the late 1960's

While he was in training, David and a number of his friends would often visit me and my family when on leave. They would bring sleeping bags and often bunked down around our apartment in Whitby. One of his friends was an East Indian prince sent to Canada for officer training due to the excellent training available in Canada. Some mornings when I got up, I would find a note on my counter that said, "Gone for the day sightseeing with the mates and taken the kids with us." My children adored their uncle and always looked forward to his visits.

David also had learned to play the bagpipes. He had a friend in the Oshawa's GM Pipe Band that taught him how to use the chanter, and Grandpa sent him a set of bagpipes from Scotland. Before moving to his regiment, he would often play the pipes outside our house on Burns Street in Whitby, marching back and forth on the front lawn. Many neighbours would come over to listen and applaud. One day, one neighbour objected to what he called "a wail of noise" and phoned the police. Unfortunately for him, the police chief was Scottish and a friend of the family, and the complainer managed to slink away after threats of jail to anyone who would dare to criticize good Highland music. Back in his regiment, he was unable to play the pipes because officers don't, but he kept it up in his spare time and continued to play in a number of pipe bands after leaving the army.

The skirl of bagpipes and the beat of the drum preceded Lieut. David G. Jack and his bride as they left Our Lady of Perpetual Help Church in Halifax recently, and marched under the arch of claymores regimental wedding of an officer of the Black Watch prior to their disbanding and one of the last appearances of officers of that historic regiment in full regalia.

Lieut. David G. Jack is and Mrs. T. Jones of Cape Breton. Best man was Capt. (Dr) George Fraser, brother-in-law of the bride and the ushers included Capt. Alex. Miller also of Chateauguay. Mrs. George Fraser, sister of the bride was matron of ho-

David and Anne's wedding: the last Scottish military wedding May 1970

David met his wife, Anne, while stationed in Nova Scotia. Anne's brother-in-law was David's best friend (he was a doctor with the Black Watch) and had introduced David to his wife's sister. David was smitten, and they were married in Halifax in May 1970 at the Royal Artillery Park, the last Scottish military wedding of an officer of the Black Watch before Canada disbanded them.

He and his wife moved to British Columbia, eventually settling in Victoria. They have two children: David and Robert. Young David went on to marry a lovely Welsh girl, Adrienne, and together, they gave my brother four beautiful grandchildren that he absolutely dotes on just as our grandfather had cared for him.

David, Anne, David and Robert   *

David and Robert

David and Adrienne

Owen, Graeme, Lucy and Eamon

Part 2: Domestic Life

After graduation, most of my friends, like most girls in the sixties expected to get married and raise a family. Few planned careers and expected to work briefly in stores, as clerks or as waitresses, before settling down. I too wanted my own family. I was engaged to a boy for a brief time before I realized his obsessive devotion to the Catholic church. After we had discussed our relationship with his priest, who insisted we were a poor match because I was definitely evil, as I was not Catholic, I took offense and handed back his ring.

Shortly after, I met the love of my life. Garry Patrick Hachie was everything I wanted; we had similar dreams and expectations and eventually planned to make it official. My mother, however, was of a different mind. Her objections to our union were due to the fact that his father was the town drunk and his family was considered low class. She refused to give my birth certificate to me so we could get a marriage license.

Almost a year later, I became pregnant, and Garry and I were delighted. My mother wasn't. She made me wear an old-fashioned girdle to school to hide my small bulge. On April 7, 1962, my birthday, Mom and Dad told me to get into the car for a "birthday" trip. They drove in silence until we pulled into a large gated estate in Port Colburn. There was a huge mansion, elaborate garden with marble statues, and a well-kept pond and grounds. We were ushered into a large room near the front door. I met an elegant lady by the name of Miss Herrig, who was the administrator of the estate. She told me that I was going to live there now. My parents left without a word. I was apparently in "Armagh"—a home for unwed mothers.

There was a wing of bedrooms, with two girls sharing a room, large bathrooms, a nurse's bed sitting room, a huge dining room, which seated about twenty-five girls, lounges, a music room, and a kitchen. The cook worked six days a week, and her husband was the grounds-keeper. They lived in a private apartment on the top floor, and so did Miss Herrig. All of us shared housekeeping duties: dusting, sweeping, and so on, as well as taking turns cooking on the cook's day off. She always left a casserole to be heated for the main meal and left break-fast and lunch to us. I always made French toast for breakfast and grilled cheese sandwiches and mushroom soup for lunch. There were always platters of fresh fruit and cheese trays. We weren't limited to the grounds and could go out anywhere we wanted, as long as we signed in and out. We were very well cared for. Our needs, clothing, schoolwork, and everything we required were met. Visitors were welcome. Garry came regularly and often prepared a picnic or barbecue to visit the park and enjoy our company together. He had a good job and had put a deposit down on the flat in Oshawa.

Mom came to visit once. She brought a sandwich for me, and we sat in the car down by the lake, a half a block away. She spent the whole time crying about how I ruined her life and how embarrassed she was. She had a social service worker come to visit me with papers to sign giving up my baby. I refused to sign them. Mom wrote me a letter saying I was to give up my child and they had made arrangements for me to go to England where my uncle would take me to Paris for art school and find me a place to live. I told her no!

On September 4, 1962, our son Robert Donald Hachie was born, and after a week, I was discharged to Armagh. I was supplied with a complete layette for the baby by Miss Herrig, and Garry picked us up and to go to our new home in Oshawa.

After a couple of weeks settling into our flat, Mom relented and finally gave me my birth certificate. At the time of our birth, all the documents showed the names of our parents, where they lived and worked, and the date of their marriage. To my surprise, they were married on January 4, 1943, just four months before we were born. I guess David and I were really premature! Her behaviour towards me was purely hypocritical.

Garry built a two-bedroom apartment in the basement of his mother's (Nanna) house. After I had our second child, Richard Todd Hachie, he built cupboards, a beautiful full bathroom, a dining room, a living room, and a roomy kitchen, even though he had had no construction training. We had what I considered (and still do) a perfect marriage. We shared our deepest thoughts. We had one bank shared account: he brought home his paycheck and I sold paintings and occasionally baby sat for friends, and all our income went to the bank. Groceries were paid by check, we planned together any and all expenditures, and he would make sure all bills were paid.

PAINTING PRESENTED TO HAWLEY

One of three paintings commissioned by Whitby Town Council

Ricky, Robbie, and Doreen

Richard (we called him Ricky) was a sickly child, frequently getting croup and requiring hospital care. After our daughter, Doreen Elizabeth Hachie, arrived we decided to buy a house. We decided that it was time for me to get a job to help with expenses. I applied to the Whitby Psychiatric Hospital, hoping to get a position in laundry, housekeeping, or the kitchens. When being interviewed, it was noted that I had a five option high school diploma, and suggested that with my education, I could be accepted in the nursing program. When I said I was mainly interested in earning a living because we had just purchased a house, they told me I would be paid for the course and also my uniforms would be provided. I started in the nursing program the following week.

The first week of class we had to memorize the name and location of every bone, muscle, and organ in the human body. So many things to go wrong! I was really surprised the human race survives. Who knew we were mostly water? As weeks and months flew by, we learned by hands on patient care, applying what we learned in the classroom. To start, each student was given one patient to care for. My first patient was a gentleman amputee in a wheelchair. He was quite adept at dressing himself and seemed a pleasant man. My first full day with him started

My Graduation from Ontario School of Nursing

at seven a.m., and I couldn't locate him. In the early morning hours, he had arisen, dressed, and wheeled himself into the hallway to have a cigarette. It took a while for the busy staff, who had been trying to get some fifty patients up, to realize he had set himself on fire. By the time they got the flames under control, it was too late. I was given another patient who was a non-smoker.

My studies, homework, and housework at home were exhausting, but Garry went over and above helping me with the kids, even though he put in a full day's work himself. He always said we were a team. After I graduated from the Ontario School of Nursing, life returned to a normal speed.

The Bunnies on parade

As a couple, we always seem to be on the same page and discussed everything relating to the kids, housework, and shopping. There was never a need to argue about anything. We joined the Whitby Arts Club, of which I became a director of activities. We were all strictly volunteers, and everyone pitched in to make the club a success. Garry did a lot of work setting up displays and, one summer, built an entire train on wheels so we could participate in the town's yearly parade. The train (Whitby Arts was located in an old railway building) was loaded with all our children, some dressed as engineers, and following a bunny theme that had warranted a lot of news coverage, Garry dressed up as a rabbit from head to toe.

David Mark Hachie was born on May 17, 1971. At this time, Garry was having thoughts about our marriage, as he hadn't been feeling "normal" or "whole" for many years. We had a number of gay friends, and after many conversations with them, he realized that a gay lifestyle appealed to him. We decided together that we should separate so he could explore his options. He would follow a gay lifestyle for a month before deciding whether to choose his family or his male friends, but I told him not both. The house was sold, and we parted ways after which I discovered he'd cleaned out our bank account and taken the car, which he'd promised to leave me after he'd bought another. I found out that he'd used the family car as a trade in for a sports car.

After three or four years, his very close-knit relatives and family, including his parents and us, had never received any word from him, which left everything in limbo. I hired a reputable private investigating company to find or at least locate him. After an extremely exhausting search, they felt there was a distinct belief that he had passed away quite likely from AIDS, which had become rampant in the early seventies.

David Mark Hachie

I dated a number of men, including a couple of longer relationships, that ended when I turned down their marriage proposals. I just didn't feel ready to exchange my name yet. I settled for a much older man, named Al Heffering, whom I decided, knew his sexuality, was separated, and had seven grown-up children. I never questioned why his five daughters disclaimed him as their father, deducing it was the parting of their parents' marriage. He had a very controlling personality, liked to be the centre of attention, and was a notorious liar, making outrageous claims to fame, like hinting that he was associated with the mafia.

Alison Logan Heffering

All the leases of the homes we had occupied through our marriage were in my name, which I found odd but expected, as he had filed for bankruptcy after giving absolutely everything, from his house and car furnishings to all his shares of stocks in Canadian Tire (he worked there for over forty years), to his ex-wife as a divorce settlement. We had a lovely daughter, Alison Logan Heffering, together after he told me he had a vasectomy. He then came up with a ridiculous lie that the doctor had given him a shot that reversed the vasectomy.

I paid all the bills by working two jobs for most of the twenty-six years we were together. He purchased high-end clothing for me (he said it made him look good) and spent lavishly on dining and entertaining friends. In all our years together, he spent nary a dime on my children, excluding Alison of course. When he made demands of me and after a number of threats, I ignored him and threatened him with police intervention.

When he tried to intervene in my business, I kicked him to the curb with absolutely no regrets. He died a few years later of cancer. No one attended his funeral—not even the mafia!

With all the turmoil, I had experienced in previous years, I was quite taken with my new admirer. Kenneth (Ken) George Friesen had an apparently good job and showered me with love and attention. We were married July 6, 2000, in the presence of my children, his two children, and a few close friends. I had no idea that he had been fired from his job the day before we tied the knot.

I also had no idea that the water bottle he was constantly filling during the day was actually straight vodka. I was very busy with my business and trusted him to pay the bills after giving him cash. I had no idea he was indulging with his "water bottles" and not paying any bills. He had also approached my friends, asking for loans because "I needed the money but was too embarrassed to come to them." After losing my house and car to his debt, I had enough and kicked him out. He died two years later in a boarding house in Oshawa, half a block from the liquor store, of alcohol poisoning. A totally wasted life! Over a span of the four years that we were together, I have about one hundred letters written by him, telling me how much he loved me and that he would never drink again.

Lynda Locke

With my other children moved out, my daughter, Alison and I settled into a lovely town house in North Oshawa, and I started my life again. I gave up my business of caring for the elderly because the house I had rented was not safe for my patients. I was hoping to reopen in a more suitable location. I kept one patient with me: Lynda was a severely mentally- and physically-challenged woman with a mind of a three-year-old. She who had been abandoned by her mother and spent most of her life in nursing homes. She was considered a part of my family and was always welcomed in the homes of my children and friends. I was responsible for her care for over thirty years.

We lived in the town house for a little over two years when I received a phone call from my mother saying she had given been one month's notice to vacate the apartment she had shared with Dad in Thornhill for thirty-five years. She told me to come and get them and find a home suitable for all of us.

Mom had been diagnosed with thyroid cancer two years prior. Every day, I had driven to Thornhill and taken her to Sunnybrook Hospital for radiation therapy. She had come down with a treatable cancer because she'd visited her doctor weekly (no appointment) for years with every ailment known to man. The doctor, who had the patience of the saint, gave up ordering tests until by accident discovered the gigantic swelling in her neck. After surgery, she had radiation treatment. After her constant complaining, insulting the doctors and nurses treating her, and being totally non-compliant, the hospital had to give her lower doses of radiation and hope for the best. In a year, the cancer returned in her lungs, and the doctors agreed that treatment would be useless because she was such a difficult patient.

It took me a couple weeks to locate a house in South Oshawa to accommodate Mom, Dad, Alison, and me. We required a bungalow because Dad was completely blind, and the house had an apartment in the basement for Alison. Sadly, I had to relocate Linda to a nursing home in Pickering because I couldn't expose her to my mother's abuse.

David flew in from Victoria, B.C., to help them move and to offer me his support. He and his family had actually moved out west to get away from our mother. Diana, as usual, didn't help. Although a couple of days prior to the move, she had come to retrieve a number of items from the apartment that she wanted, like the carved tables, tools, and a lot of things she thought were valuable. Dad stopped her from taking the antique grandfather clock that had been in our family for generations. The actual move was horrendous. Mom insisted her bed be the last to load because she needed to rest and expected the bed and linen to be set up immediately upon arrival at the new location. The apartment owners were absolutely delighted that they were moving because Mom had been an annoying tenant and they waved the two-month notice usually required.

Diana showed up at the new house after we got them settled to get some cheques from Mom and, as she usually did, asked Dad if she could get her inheritance then. The answer was no! My dad said, "We aren't even dead yet!"

Mom was an alcoholic and always had been, usually blaming the empty Scotch bottles on Dad's drinking and neighbours dropping in for a "wee drink." In Thornhill, they lived directly beside the liquor store and were upset to find that the liquor store in Oshawa was a couple blocks away.

Diana visited for Thanksgiving and told Mom that she and Dad could move to a nursing home a few miles from her and mentioned that it was next to a plaza with a restaurant, liquor store, and a convenience store. Diana said she would be able to look after their finances for them. I lost my temper because of everything we had endured having to locate suitable accommodation for them on short notice. The move with Diana would be for all the wrong reasons. Dad told me to just ignore Mom because she would forget about everything by the following day and he had no intention of moving. Mom remained difficult; she was diagnosed with dementia and would walk up to the liquor store and ask strangers to drive her home because she was too weak to walk home due to her advanced years. She refused to let me drive her so that she could hide where she was going; I took to following her to keep her safe. Dad's health improved with proper nutrition. Mom usually ate most of his meals from his plate in Thornhill. He was happier to be able to shave, wash, and be dressed properly with care. I took him monthly to the CNIB Club for blind seniors, where members and family were entertained. He was a very congenial, endearing man and made many friends there.

A couple of months after Mom and Dad had settled, I became ill. Alison took me to the hospital where an ultrasound found a blockage (tumour) in my abdomen. I was on a diet of fluids only and started feeling better. I made the poor choice of flying to Calgary to be with my daughter Doreen and family for the birth of her second child. I was hungry and ate probably the best sandwich I ever had, made by Doreen, and became really ill. I was taken by ambulance to hospital where the doctor there told me I had to immediately return to Ontario.

David flew in from B.C. and escorted me back to Ontario. I missed the birth of my grandson. The doctor had been sent documents from Calgary, and Robbie, who had escorted me to his office, was instructed to take me to the hospital immediately. Alison was going to have to supervise Mom and Dad for a while. Mom was quite capable of making her own tea but was angry because "she needed taken care of." My condition became critical in the hospital, and the family were told that possibly I may not survive. I had emergency surgery and a portion of my intestines were removed and after a month recovered enough to go home. Robbie escorted me home. While I was trying gingerly to get into the house, Mom was in the kitchen making tea and started yelling at me for leaving her to cope on her own. When told that I had almost died, she yelled, "You should have died. Why didn't you?"

I continued to care for my parents to the best of my ability until Mom passed away on December 13, 2007. Dad's only remark was "Hmm, thirteen was always my lucky number." As requested, she received no funeral and her ashes were taken to Scotland's Loch Lomond to be put under the newly planted Rowen tree (her favourite) on a hillside in a cemetery overlooking the Loch. Our cousin Christine took the remains for us, as she often went home for visits. A sad end to a life that created misery for everyone she knew. Her last words to me were, "I actually do love you!"

Dad (Robert William Hannah Jack b1913-2008)
Mom (Agnes Graham McInlay Jack nee Forgan b 1918- 2007)

At the age of ninety-five, Dad passed away peacefully four months later on April 23, 2008, after a life of honour and dedication to his family and many friends. We treasure his memory every day.

Chapter 7

Nursing (My Chosen Field)

Part 1: The Way It Was and I Saw It; the Way It Is as I See It

For decades, the Whitby Psychiatric Hospital was a self-contained marvel. Over one thousand patients, two large infirmaries—one male, the other female, for the aged and ill—two large admission buildings (east and west), a large building for patients requiring constant supervision, numerous "cottages" with open doors for stable patients, and an award-winning farm, with a modern barn to house cattle and pigs and acres of chickens and coops. The hospital was surrounded by cornfields and apple orchards. The cottages had a number of vegetable gardens that patients tended for themselves. On the farm road, there were cottages for staff with families and smaller homes, where some of the doctors and their families resided, scattered around the grounds. Buses made regular trips to take kids to school.

There was an efficient laundry room and a main kitchen. Several dining rooms in various areas, and each large locked building had its own kitchen area and dining room. Many patients arose at four a.m. to a hearty breakfast of eggs, bacon, cereal, unending toast, juice, and coffee or tea before heading out to the fields to gather eggs, help plow fields, or tend to the farm animals. Large garbage cans in each building were kept and emptied of food scraps and leftovers to feed the pigs. There was a main office building and a school of nursing. All in all, a totally self-contained, efficient set up.

Then a general hospital (funded mainly by residents of Whitby) was built on the property, complete with a modern maternity wing and nursery. However, that was when the government, in its usual wisdom, changed the necessity of having too many hospitals per capita. Ajax had just built a hospital too. The Whitby Hospital, known as the J. O. Ruddy Hospital, never opened for the purpose of serving Whitby residents. Then, in the early 1970s, the government declared that a general hospital couldn't occupy the same acreage as a farm. Goodbye farm and home-grown food! The barn burnt down in 1976 and the patients lost their purpose and will. Ready-made "food" was shipped in for the patients. Cottages were torn down, and patients moved into group homes in town. Many old homes took in large numbers of patients, squeezing several into small rooms with the odd blanket on a cot. Patients were given a breakfast of cereal and coffee in the morning, then a bag with usually a peanut butter sandwich, and escorted outside, regardless of the weather, until supper time. The owners of the houses receive the patients ODSP or CPP cheques. A new building was erected, serving a maximum of two hundred patients and the school of nursing closed. Nursing students entered colleges where they learned patient care via computers rather than hands on. This was called "advancement" and, in the end, government folly costing millions and a definite decline in the mental health issues for hundreds of displaced patients. That was the way it was.

Long-term care homes started sprouting up for families who could no longer care for aging parents at home because two incomes were now needed to make ends meet due to the ever-rising cost of living. An example was Ballycliffe in Ajax, offering a lovely spacious one- or two-bedroom suite with sturdy furniture and efficient activity program for all residents, which included outside bowling and a monthly family night with live entertainment and a time to bring loved ones together. Patient care and comfort were of the utmost priority. A hairdresser was paid a salary by the administration, avoiding extra costs for the families. Residents helped make cookies and cupcakes so everyone could participate in supplying munchies for mid-morning tea and coffee breaks. That was the way it was!

Times had changed! The golden idol reared. Money and greed took precedence. Large conglomerates took over our hospitals and LTC Homes "making a buck" was the rallying cry. Residents, unless they could afford a private or semiprivate room, were crammed into a four-bedroom suite, limiting privacy and storage space. Staff members were reduced, medical supplies were in short supply, and the meals were of low standard, providing non-healthy and cheaper pasta, rice, and corn products. I know of one home that had a cook that prepared meals for breakfast and lunch, and high school students came in after school to reheat supper. In the winter, very often at Sunnycrest in Whitby, that was spaghetti and ketchup, and in the warmer months, patients were given a square cube of Jell-o with a carrot slice or a pea in it, a spoon of cottage cheese on lettuce, and maybe a slice of canned peaches or, if they were lucky, a slice of cooked ham. No mid-morning snacks unless a visit was prearranged by a health inspector. Then a trolley of juice or coffee with a biscuit would miraculously appear. They also had an extremely short supply of linens and blankets. As most residents were incontinent and linen unavailable, staff used coats from closets to cover the residents.

Scepter Home on the outskirts Uxbridge, situated along a deserted dirt road surrounded by forest and swamp, was home to mostly aggressive psychiatric patients left over from Whitby who had the unfortunate habit of getting old. Those were the lost souls with severe mental illnesses and no family or relatives to care for them. The majority of staff were local farm girls with no training, and the building itself was dilapidated, with only two bathrooms to serve some fifty patients, which didn't really matter because most of the male patients just urinated anywhere. Housekeeping staff were nonexistent. The stench of urine of was prevalent. The owners of this "hell hole" were the two Martino brothers and a sister, frequently associated with the mafia. I assume the home was a tax shelter. One day, without notifying staff, a number of buses transported the patients to another LTC in Bowmanville's Main Street, where an addition had been added to accommodate them. Scepter was razed and no longer exists. The Martino family must have found the venture quite profitable because they have branched out to running funeral homes and golf and country clubs. Money does truly buy prestige and control.

Rosebank Villa was purchased by a group of East Indians with absolutely no medical knowledge. They immediately reduced staff and privileges for the residents. The former administrator (a doctor), residents, and many families removed their elderly loved ones because the care for them became inadequate. That was the way it was.

After graduating from the school of nursing, I remained an employee at the Whitby Psychiatric Hospital for sixteen years, with six weeks off for pregnancies. At those times, I chose to resign and returned as a part-time worker. As a part-time nurse, I could work in any location and any shifts I wanted. I was called to work every day, so I usually worked a number of double shifts (three p.m. to eleven p.m. and eleven p.m. to seven a.m.) every week and would take a few days off in between. I was earning more than the full-time staff and worked the locations of my choice. I liked medical units and admitting units the best, as they were challenging but interesting at the same time.

One afternoon in admitting, which was a locked ward, a large number of visitors came in accompanied by administration staff. As we often had visitors, we paid no attention and resumed our duties. I was approached by a gentleman who asked me to unlock the door so he could leave—a request often made by newly admitted patients. I told him I was not authorized to open the door, so he told me he was the health minister and had to leave. I replied, "I am pleased to meet you, but I can't unlock the door." He was insistent about being the minister of health, so I told him I could introduce him to two Jesus Christs and Queen Victoria that we were also entertaining at that time. It turned out that the gentleman actually was the minister of health!

One of our patients was a lovely lady who had been in a horrendous marital relationship and suffered a mental breakdown. She never spoke and never interacted with the staff or other patients. After several weeks of no communication, we decided to allow her to have a walk outdoors for some fresh air, accompanied of course. I volunteered and we strolled slowly on the large path that meandered through the hospital grounds. Unfortunately, Canada geese had left their mark with millions of white blobs on the walkway, making it necessary to constantly tried to avoid them. Suddenly, my patient stopped, looked thoughtfully up to the sky, and remarked, "I'm really glad that cows can't fly!" She was finally on her way to recovery.

In the late fall, many of our patients were readmitted to the hospital after spending their summers living as panhandlers on the streets. They were escorted to the tub room where they were stripped, groomed, and deloused. They were supplied with "new" clothes and given medical care, as well as some decent nourishment. One enterprising patient returned every year asking for dental care. There was a dentist on the hospital grounds with very high-end expensive equipment and often had state-of-the-art dentures made for individuals requiring them. This one patient, every year, had his usual complaint of losing his dentures, and we found out that he was actually selling them on the street when he was discharged. We noticed that he never used his dentures himself because he wasn't used to wearing them. Thousands of taxpayers' dollars went out the door every spring!

A lot of patients had town privileges and would go into Whitby or Oshawa for the day, many hanging around the gas stations to beg from customers. Frequently, they would take the taxi to the hospital to keep evening curfew and told the drivers to charge the hospital. After some years, and hundreds of dollars of taxi bills later, the hospital administrators approached all the taxi services in the Durham region and told them that no longer would the hospital be held accountable for their service. Staff had to show identification to prove they were employees not patients every time they wanted to grab a taxi to work.

The medical units housed the very elderly, mostly dementia patients and the occasional person recovering from an illness or a broken limb. They were relatively quiet at night. We routinely checked for incontinence and patient comfort throughout the night. One elderly lady was known to be extremely vocal and disruptive if she had soiled herself and would wake up everyone else on the ward. We would have to take her and the bed out into the hallway to tend to her needs and tried to calm everyone she had awakened. Hers was the only bed we would avoid at night because she would start screaming and throwing everything from her bed if she was disturbed. One morning, we started our morning care, thankful for a quiet night, when we realized the noisy disruptive patient had passed away. Due to the fact that she was cold and rigor mortis (stiffening) had set in, we realized she had probably died during the previous shift. We quickly placed her body into a tub of very warm water before calling the coroner. Her skin temperature had risen and the doctor was somewhat baffled at her condition but thankfully didn't ask for any explanations.

I enjoyed working at the hospital but felt the need to branch out to other ventures.

Part 3: Comfort Cottage

Headline from the Oshawa Times

After many years working as a charge nurse in the Durham regions Long Term Care Homes, I was so angry and disillusioned with the atrocities committed against our most valuable citizens, I decided to do something to change their circumstances. Keeping in mind that the entire province of Ontario is probably the same, I can only speak of my experiences in the long-term homes I had been sadly associated with. In the 1990s, I opened up a special care facility for disabled adults and seniors. With a license from the Town of Whitby, I started Comfort Cottage. I rented a house in the heart of the town that required a lot of cleaning, as it had previously been a "drug den." I was given decent furniture from the very generous Salvation Army and got a number of proper hospital beds from the Oshawa Hospital that their housekeeping and maintenance department had discarded. Most needed minor repairs and cleaning. I got a lot of medical supplies, like over bed tables, night stands, bedpans, and so on, from a dear friend Bill Link, who had been accumulating equipment from closed nursing homes to distribute among anyone who needed medical equipment. After I purchased air mattresses, sheep skins, and linen, I was in business.

Me and some of the Residents of Comfort Cottage

My first patients actually came from Rosebank Villa in Pickering, where the families weren't happy with the care given to their loved ones and found out from staffed there where I had gone. Rosebanks' new owners tried suing me for stealing their patients, but a gentle reminder from a lawyer reminded them that their residents were not prisoners and could live where they chose. They dropped their suit. I only had seven beds, but it was a start!

A lot of my residents came from the Bowmanville Hospital social workers. They were in the final stages of MS, which left them severely disabled but very alert and needing total care. Most nursing homes in the region are reluctant to take such patients because they require more staff to meet their needs. I had a lot of final year nursing students who were completing their clinical training coming in because they got the opportunity to use the skills they had learned in the classroom. The probation office started sending people that had not committed serious crimes but given a sentence of community service for a variety of hours. I put them to work: mowing the lawn, doing general cleanup, and general repairs. After completing their community service, many returned as volunteers. Grade 11 students also arrived to do community service required by the school board. I always started them off with a contest of riding a wheelchair around the block. They accepted the challenge with enthusiasm until they arrived back exhausted but with a better understanding of what it would be like to live the rest of their lives in a wheelchair.

Mealtimes were an interesting time. Breakfast was resident's choice. Some liked bacon and eggs; others were partial to pancakes or French toast. One lady liked her Scotch porridge with cream and salt, like we made back home in Scotland; it was always their choice. Leftovers from supper meals went into a big pot on the stove, and after adding a few noodles or rice, the soups were always a big hit for lunch. Whether lasagna, stews, roasts, or chicken dishes, supper was always a vote, and amazingly everyone always agreed with the decisions. We had a full-time doctor who was semi-retired and was on call 24/7, although he often dropped by for a visit and a cup of tea ,as did several town council members.

The Whitby transit buses (one bus being wheelchair accessible) made a regular stop at Comfort Cottage to make it easier for the residents accompanied by nursing staff, of course, to go shopping in Oshawa. Patricia, one of our residents, liked to go to the Scarborough town centre, so I would lift her all ninety-pound frame into the car, put her wheelchair in my trunk, and go for an afternoon of shopping. One afternoon, I found the parking lot really full and searched for a handicap spot (I had a sticker on my car). When I finally spotted one, I immediately drove in just before another gentleman who wanted the same space did. I got out of my car to retrieve the wheelchair when the man got out of his car and started yelling at me for taking a handicap spot. Patricia was a tiny woman, and he hadn't noticed her in the car. I put my hands on my hips and loudly yelled back at him, "How'd dare you yell at me. You have no idea what my handicap is. I happen to be blind!" He muttered apologies and quickly drove away. Patricia wondered how long it would take him to realize a blind person was incapable of driving.

I made it my mission to care for my residents with love and respect and make their remaining years as happy and comfortable as possible. I didn't make any money, even though I charged less than LTC homes, but I received and gained immense satisfaction and pride in what I had accomplished.

After a number of years operating Comfort Cottage, a representative from Ontario Hydro paid us a visit. They had noticed that our hydro bill was far above average for the neighbourhood and suspected a possible grow operation or default in the home's construction. The gentleman tested all the rooms, doors, windows, and roof and, to everyone's amazement, found absolutely no insulation whatsoever in the building, causing a tremendous loss of heat and very high hydro bills, especially in the colder months. A young man sentenced to community service by the courts was employed by a reputable furnace maintenance company and offered to clean our furnace and filter to improve efficiency. He was alarmed at what he found and advised strongly on replacing the entire furnace, as he felt it was dangerous to the residence and occupants. The fire department also suggested a replacement before winter. I approached the landlord with my concerns. He was a gentleman who lived off the proceeds of people who were on ODSP (disability) and social assistance in a large number of unkempt houses throughout Whitby and

Oshawa and had no intention of replacing anything. After many heated discussions, I felt it prudent and safer to relocate to a different location.

Most of my long-term residents had passed away, so I spent a great deal of effort trying to locate a suitable building to carry on elsewhere. I had a wealthy friend willing to put up a great deal of money as a silent partner to accomplish a move, but that was when my husband, Al, came to me with a solution. A long-time friend was very interested in the business and wanted to foot the bill. He was in the construction business and could easily meet all my needs. After several appointments were cancelled at the last minute to meet with Al's backer, I was becoming a little suspicious. I knew Al lied about everything, but this enterprise affected our family life. I had his friend's name and business card, so I phoned him myself, as Al had always conversed with him. The "friend" actually existed but many years had past since he had spoke with Al and he had absolutely no knowledge of any plans to start a business. That was the end of Comfort Cottage, my dreams, and my relationship. Evil knows no boundaries.

Chapter 8

Nursing Associations

Many years at Comfort Cottage opened up many opportunities to teach a variety of options related to the health field. I took on the task of teaching the PSW course for the Ontario government adult retraining program. Most of my students were women who, due to marital problems, very little education, and no work history, had ended up on government assistance and were attempting to become self-sufficient while working at an honourable job. As well as learning to care for mainly disabled patients and, in particular, seniors in nursing homes and those requiring supervision and assistance at home, the students were sometimes required to do light housekeeping and meal preparations. I was surprised at the number of younger women that were incapable of boiling water. Apparently, they had never been taught to cook or clean from early childhood. The classes were a challenge, but hopefully, my teaching produced higher functioning adults who could now be proud of their learned knowledge and apply it to future endeavors.

Many of my students completed clinical hours at Comfort Cottage to further their knowledge of hands-on care, as a number of nursing students from college did.

I was aware of an incident regarding a theft of a large sum of money, stolen from an incapacitated senior. It was a case of elder abuse, which can take many forms, from theft to physical, mental, and/or emotional abuse committed by family members, caregivers, and even strangers. There was a problem with the justice system. It was not familiar with the mechanics of abuse of the elderly and disabled, and each county had a vastly different way of dealing with such serious problems. I was approached by the assistant crown attorney to inform them, as a consultant, on exactly who, how, and where the variety of elder abuse takes place and to set standards in Ontario on sentencing perpetrators of this crime. The information was passed to the police, crown attorneys, and judges. I was called by the crown as an expert witness of elder abuse on two court cases involving theft of money and household belongings and had the satisfaction in the knowledge that the two defendants were given hefty the jail sentences.

Grade 11 students in Ontario are required to put in a number of hours of community service, and because I'd had students from the local high schools, I was asked to talk at Henry Street High School in Whitby on psychiatry. My daughter's teacher had assigned some work to her class in sociology, but I realized the information she had been taught was wrong. The teacher explained that he was a math teacher, knew nothing about psychiatry, and had been given the job because he had extra class hours available. I arranged to speak to the students in my daughter's Grade 11 class in the classroom itself for, what I expected to be, a thirty-five-minute session. Due to my busy schedule, I made no preparations beforehand and found out through the school that classes were actually ninety minutes long and that I had to keep the attention of all Grade 11 students, over one hundred of them.

When my charges were seated at desks, windowsills, and on the floor, I wrote on the blackboard a large number of names off the top of my head and asked my audience to identify them. I had written the names of well-known mass murderers and serial killers. That got the students' attention while I explained the psychiatry. We went on to the variety of the different forms of schizophrenia and how to identify people with mental health issues. When the bell rang for the end of the class, the students remained seated, still asking me questions, and had to be told several times that the class was over.

A lot of high schools have a career day and each student must visit three classes about their future career interests. There was a fireman, policemen, teacher, nurse, dentist, and a large variety of other occupations to choose from. I was representing gerontology. My first class of students, to my surprise, turned out to be attended by an unusual number of boys. I found this rather strange because teenage boys are rarely interested in the subject of senior's well-being. When the third class arrived, again with a large attendance of boys, I inquired as to what was going on to attract so many young men. They sheepishly told me that they had to choose three subjects, we're not interested in becoming firemen or such, and had no idea what gerontology was, so decided to give it a try. At least, I'd taught them that eventually they were going to get old and to keep that in mind when dealing with seniors—and to learn from their elders and give them the love and respect they themselves will require one day.

Chapter 9

Bits and Tidbits!

On the set of Mafia Princess

When I was working at the psychiatric hospital as a part-time nurse, I was able to take any number of days or evenings off, especially after working three or four double shifts in a row. During the early 1980s, my daughter was looking for a summer job and applied to a talent agency hiring film and movie extras. There was a great deal of movies being made in Ontario at the time, so I accompanied her to a large meeting of potential "extras." They were mainly looking for adult shoppers, parents, restaurant employees, and customers—in other words, the regular everyday people. I spent many hours on movie sets as a nurse (I had my own uniform), a waitress, and a call girl (due to my long blonde hair). I was also in period films because I could fit into gowns from the turn of the century. I ended up in over one hundred films and TV shows, working with such stars as Sophia Loren, Charles Bronson, John Ritter, Brad Pitt, and a horde of other celebrities.

Most shows were filmed in all sorts of weather. I vividly remember standing on street corners dressed as a prostitute, with a minimal amount of clothing on, in a snowstorm or pouring rain. With large spotlights, police, and camera crews standing nearby, it never ceased to amaze me how many cars pulled over with men inside asking me, "How much?". My standard answer was usually, "You can't afford me, Buster!"

Movies are rarely filmed in the order that the script was written. We usually had no idea what the "story" was about, just were told where to walk, run, or whether to react happy, sad, outraged, angry, or uninterested. Most scenes were "shot" over and over to get the desired results that the director envisioned. One film called for smokers. The scene was for a TV series making fun of the new government law regarding designated smoking areas in buildings. The scene was just outside an elevator. Large signs with arrows were pointing down the walls and across the floor to a large circle in the middle of the hallway marked "smoking area!" About thirty of us extras crammed into the circle, lit up our cigarettes (provided by crew), and started smoking away like mad while two of the "stars" walked by, paying no attention to us. The glitch came when the two actors passed us and they couldn't hold in their laughter. We ended up doing the scene over and over until they could control their emotions. Meanwhile, we were all dying from the many packs of cigarettes we had to smoke before the director yelled, "Cut! Cigarette break everyone!"

One weekly series on TV was about "the guardian angels of New York." In one episode, the actors come across a woman leaving a church service who goes into cardiac arrest. I was the unfortunate patient but spent an entire day off set, teaching the actors how to perform resuscitation (CPR). I had assumed they would "fake" the procedure on camera, but my assumption was wrong. It did not help when they dropped me off the gurney while putting me into an ambulance and had to repeat the entire scene over again. After that, I felt that I actually needed CPR!

One of the rioting scenes in the iconic *Police Academy* movie had the crew spending a day prior to filming carefully spreading assorted garbage all over the alleyways and sidewalks for a realistic effect. After all, the movie was supposed to be portraying New York City. They filmed an entire morning of total chaos until the director cut for our lunch break. When we returned to the set to finish filming the scene, we found that the diligent Toronto Works Department had cleaned up all of our carefully placed debris. An extra day was spent repeating the garbage detail.

For a decade, I continued with "extra" work and, for the most part, enjoyed it immensely. There was less work available in the summer because hundreds of school teachers, if having the summer off, took the jobs from the people that had only "extra" work to make a living. I started becoming bored with this extra-curricular activity anyway, and when I broke my leg, I was forced to find other "amusement."

One of my coworkers on set was a gentleman who also ran an up-and-coming catering service. He asked me to take over a management position, as I would only be required to sit at a desk, do the books, and interview potential clients needing our service. After nine weeks in a cast, with only crutches to get around, I continued with other aspects of business related to catering. I hired the staff and organized the food, liquor, and permits for each job. Sometimes, there would be five weddings on the same day. We often supplied the military banquets and Whitby Town council luncheons, as well as teacher meetings and some house parties.

Not all weddings went well, however. A smaller wedding, requiring less staff, was held in a hall in Whitby. They wanted to avoid the taxes, so were going to pay for the nuptials in cash. After dinner, the bride's father went into the cloakroom to retrieve the money from his jacket pocket to pay me and found it was gone. All the guests were family and close friends; so naturally, they suspected the catering staff of the theft. They took up a collection to pay their bill, and the following day, the father of the bride showed up at my office to apologize to us. Apparently, a friend of the groom had offered to take the photos and video of the wedding. And that evening after the happy couple left for their honeymoon, everyone sat around to view the video. To everyone's surprise, the camera caught the bride's uncle sneaking into the cloakroom and removing the money from his brother's pocket. He was one of the viewers and watched himself caught in the act.

One of the most interesting jobs was a special birthday party celebration for the elderly father of the Japanese ambassador. The embassy was in Hamilton. We always carried a sword with us because a lot of couples like a photo of themselves cutting the wedding cake with the sword. For the embassy party, I borrowed a sword for my father. He had been given a ceremonial sword by a general of the Japanese Army after their defeat in World War Two. Many Japanese people were in poor condition after the war. They suffered from starvation and illness. The British forces tried to help by giving them food and supplies, but the Japanese, being a proud people, refused "charity" and insisted on "paying" for the goods with personal heirlooms and whatever they had. When the Americans arrived, they just took everything as souvenirs and banned the people from owning weapons of every kind. Dad ended up with several swords, including the general's. When the elderly gentleman was being honored at his party, he asked his son to purchase the sword from me at any cost. He apparently recognized it. I apologized to the ambassador and told him the sword was not mine to sell. When I returned the sword to Dad and told him the story, he said, "Oh, why didn't you just give it to him!" That's my dad!

Another wedding that involved a sword had dire consequences for the groom. At the wedding reception, the bride proved to be a self-centered, obnoxious, spoiled brat to put it nicely. She belittled her new husband so much he escaped to the kitchen and expressed a desire to separate from his new wife and her father, who had encouraged her ill behaviour. The day after their short honeymoon, there was a photo in the newspaper showing the "happy" couple cutting their wedding cake with "our" sword. The caption read "bride's father kills newlywed husband with a sword." Apparently, their arguing continued in their own apartment, and the bridezilla phoned her father for support. He brought his own sword and ended his daughter ill-fated marriage.

On occasion, I did some short-term jobs requiring my "expertise," such as it was. One such job involved an entrepreneur who had invented and built a three-wheeled motorcycle. To attract potential investors, he asked me to train and hire young ladies to be showroom models. One of our assignments was for the grand opening of the Consumers' Gas Building on Consumers Drive in Whitby. I did have fairly strict rules for everyone while we walked around the showroom with hors d'oeuvres and wine, talking to potential customers. One rule was no talk of politics, religion, or sex. The job paid well (they also displayed a selection of my oil paintings throughout the room, as gas fireplaces and dryers and such could be boring), but I decided "modelling" was not for me after all. It was too frustrating dealing with young women with unattainable aspirations.

Around the time that the Pickering Town Centre was built, I was contacted by the Dunbarton Business Association. Apparently, the little plaza on the baseline, which had catered to the needs of all the local residents, were sorely lacking in customers due to the new large Pickering Plaza, and they asked me to come up with ideas to attract the shoppers back. My theory was to attract the children, who, in turn, would surely be accompanied by their parents. I came up with the idea of a "design a Christmas card" contest. The committee thought it was a good idea and offered prizes (bikes and such) for different age groups. I made up a number of fliers and delivered them to all the schools in the area to pass out to interested children.

I expected maybe one hundred entries, which didn't account for the laziness of teachers. The teachers all integrated my contest into their classes, so we ended up with thousands of entries. My friends helped me sort through the huge pile of pictures according to age, grade, and imaginative works. On the day of announcing the winners (which was during a snowstorm), the little Dunbarton Plaza had so many cars and people that a traffic jam ensued and the stores ran out of coffee, sandwiches, treats, and varieties of other products. The committee decided that I was too successful at the job and decided to un-hire me for future work. First time, I was fired for being too competent!

Junior group winners with their cards and librarian Thea Driesschen.

Christmas card designers

PICKERING — More ... ol. Doug won a table ... Honorable mentions ... year-old Susan Bu... grade six pupil

Chapter 10

Family Matters

Robbie, Ricky, David, Doreen and Alison

Children empower women, in particular, to succeed in life. Raising them is a lifelong quest to achieve perfection for them; hopefully, leaving the example that education, hard work, confidence in their unique abilities will produce well-adjusted young adults. Each child has their own personality, and my children are no different. Robbie, the eldest, was the instigator in our household; Ricky, the scapegoat; Doreen, the boss, relying on consequences and good judgment; David counted on the old adage "it wasn't me!"; and Alison, the youngest, did things her way, a definite mind of her own (many times out in left field!)

Ricky was a sickly child, spending a lot of time in hospital until he grew out of his many childhood illnesses. Doreen was born with a hole in her heart, requiring very delicate surgery at the age of five. Ricky, Doreen, and David also had severe eyesight problems, causing blindness apparently due to an extremely rare gene that their father and I both carried. I found that children are only as handicapped as you tell them. Where there's a will, there's a way! I am happy that my children survived to be strong, loving, and responsible adults, making me an exceptionally proud mother.

When the children were very young, my husband dropped me off at a shopping centre where I'd been charged with all the Christmas shopping while he watched the kids. We agreed that he would return to pick me up at the main doors just outside of Zellers, at six p.m. I spent the entire day trudging around the mall, lugging boxes and bags and presents. When six came, exhausted, I went to the Zellers entrance to wait for my ride. I was surprised there was a blinding snowstorm outside. It seemed an eternity before I spotted our car as it pulled up to the curb. I ran over, open the backdoor, and threw all my parcels into the back seat. I slammed the backdoor and jumped into the front passenger seat yelling, "Get me the hell out of here!" It was then that I looked over to see a total stranger behind the wheel staring at me, and with a glance behind the car, I spotted a similar vehicle with my husband sitting in it, grinning with amusement. I muttered my apologies, retrieved my parcels, and sheepishly got into our own car.

I did become quite adept at having embarrassing situations. Drinking alcohol was prohibited until the age of twenty-one in the early sixties. We could drive a car and enlist in the army but not imbibe. When I turned to twenty-one, we were invited to a GM Christmas party by friends who worked at General Motors. We all sat at long tables in the festively draped room. Directly sitting across from me was a lone gentleman, apparently alone, and he was wearing the most hideous tie I had ever seen. One of our friends asked me what I would like to drink; I had no knowledge of the wide assortments of alcoholic beverages available, so I started with vodka and orange juice, then a rye and ginger ale. I graduated to a gin and tonic, then rum and Coke, and finally finishing up with a Scotch and soda. I had no idea that overindulging in alcohol beverages had side effects. The gentleman sitting across from me continued to stare with a stupid grin on his face when my stomach rebelled and I promptly threw up all over the atrocious tie he was wearing. I was quickly escorted to the ladies' room by my friends, and when I returned to my seat, Mr. Ugly Tie was still sitting in the same place. I didn't catch his name! I hope he didn't know mine!

The very first apartment we had was in South Oshawa. It was actually a flat in the upstairs of a small house on Cordova Street. The landlord and his family with four children lived on the main floor, while we lived upstairs with a separate entrance, one bedroom, living room, kitchen, and bathroom, with a very large deep-footed tub. Unfortunately, I had contracted plantar warts on the soles of both feet, and the doctor advised me not to get my feet wet while the prescription cream he had ordered was carefully applied to the warts and covered with soft dressing. After a week, I was desperate to have a full bath, so with one of my usual "brilliant" solutions, I enclosed both feet in plastic bags tied tightly around the ankles, climbed into the tub, and started filling the tub with water. It didn't take long for me to realize that my feet were floating. I couldn't reach the drain stopper but managed to turn off the taps. Because the tub was so deep, I had to hang onto both sides to stay afloat. My housecoat was hanging behind the bathroom door, and the towel was out of reach, so calling for assistance to my landlord was out of the question. I had to wait for over an hour before my husband finally came home from work to rescue me. By that time, the water had become cold and cramps had set in to my derriere. I reluctantly went back to sponge baths until the warts disappeared.

We all managed to survive childhood, sometimes by the skin of our teeth. Robbie has owned and operated an auto shop in Whitby called Pro Street for over thirty-five years. He also builds and races cars, a dangerous sideline on its own. He has had many successes and many friends and associates. His two children, Stephen and Jacquie, are grown up and successful in their own right.

Stephen works in real estate and has a close relationship. He and Scott expect to be bound legally after the COVID-19 virus subsides. Jacquie is a beautiful woman with a delightful little boy, now eight years old. I cared for my great grandson in his early years while his mother completed her college education.

Ricky has run a successful printing business for many years in spite of his poor eyesight. He isn't as sociable as his older brother, but his close group of friends are long-term and reliable. And he has three lovely boys. The eldest, Kyle, has matured into a responsible adult and will be married shortly. Trevor, a brilliant student, is busy in medical research, and Nicholas is advancing in the workforce.

Doreen became a teacher, then returned to university to become a psychologist, specializing in autistic children. She has two children: Gillian is completing her high school year, preparing for college, and is extremely talented in the field of art. Kristian, my youngest grandchild, will be representing Canada in the next Olympics. He is completely dedicated to the martial arts and, through unrelenting practise, is at the very top of his field.

David struggles with his blindness but manages well with the support of his wife, Lee Anne, a kind and gentle woman with numerous health challenges also.

Alison is working in the film industry as security, mostly long night shifts, which she prefers. She has many close friends and an almost obsession with Star Wars, Harry Potter, and the other "cult" films. Working on the movie sets, she has become acquainted with many stars who frequently keep in touch. Alison lives in the same house with me, although with her own living quarters. In 2008, she was very badly injured in a car crash when a young man with a truck broadsided the car in which she was a passenger. Even now, she continues to suffer the pain from the injuries but relies on her many cats and pets to comfort her.

After a number of years as a widow and occasional dating, I actually jumped into the matrimonial bed for the fourth time. Gordon Rae Hart was cautioned by my brother, David, of course, but actually jumped in with me, ignoring the challenges. I call him Gord, although his two sisters and two brothers and all nephews and nieces (there are many) refer to him as "Robbie" for some unknown reason.

My family seems to be limited with the selection of names. Growing up, holidays were very confusing. Robert is the birth name of my father, my son, my nephew, and my cousin. David is the birth name of my brother, uncle, cousin, and a nephew. Richard is my son, brother-in-law, and nephew . I don't suppose it helps that I named our newly acquired eight-year-old rescue dog "Bobby."

Chapter 11

Is Our Culture Advancing or Retreating?

Part 1: Banks

I remember a time when a local bank was a place of trust, a place where your money was well looked after. You actually received generous interest rates on your savings. At a time of very few credit cards, personal cheques were used to pay our bills and even make purchases in stores. Personal cheques were free always. Somehow, slowly, things changed. Managing a bank must have become a profitable organization because banks suddenly popped up everywhere. The price of getting cheques became expensive. We get charged to deposit our hard-earned money into our accounts, and the interest rates to use their credit cards are almost criminal.

While running my special care facility, all transactions were conducted with cheques. The TD Bank close to my business had an area for businesses; it was more convenient to use that area for deposits, as the lineup for a teller was considerably shorter. At the first of every month, I would deposit a large number of cheques into my business account, then return to work to write cheques to cover the rent, household bills, and staff wages. I had no problems until I received a cheque for a utility payment marked "not cleared"! In other words, the funds were available to pay the bill, but the bank couldn't process it at that time. My inquiry was met with the explanation that all cheques at that bank were held for five business days. As it happened, I had deposited the cheques on the Friday of a long weekend, and this bank consider depositing after three p.m., marking it to the following Tuesday. They wouldn't honor cheques (even business) for a further five working days. My calculations made that eleven days altogether on a long weekend.

To avoid the same nonsense, I closed the account with TD and, after inquiries, opened my account at the Bank of Montreal across the street. They didn't hold back cheques for business accounts. For many years, everything ran smoothly until, one day, I received the utility cheque returned "not cleared." Knowing I had plenty in the account to cover all my bills, I called the bank to find out what was going on. They told me that there was a "hold" on my account and would notify me on how to proceed. A few days later, I received a special delivery letter the in the mail stating that my account was on hold due to the fact that I was "deceased." Apparently, I had died and I wasn't even given the courtesy of being informed. Being slightly enraged, I went over to the BMO, marched into the very crowded bank, held the bank's letter into the air, and yelled at the top of my lungs, "Can I have your attention please! Is there any one here that can confirm that I am alive, as I have a letter here from this bank stating my account is closed because I am dead." I then left the bank, followed by a few customers. It took almost a month to reverse the bank's mistake. I can fully understand why many seniors only use cash stashed under a mattress. Of course, the government sends the old age pension cheques by mail, and the banks charge a fee to cash them for you. A lose, lose situation all around.

Part 2: Police Services

In every barrel, there is usually at least one rotten apple, and I am sure the same is said throughout numerous Ontario and Canadian regions. I can only speak as to what I am familiar with. I have a great deal of faith and support for police and admire their dedication to serve and protect. However, I also know there are several officers in our area that don't deserve my faith in the force.

An excellent example was the young officer in a police car who stopped my friend's son at the Oshawa Shopping Centre. Warren was a young man, neatly dressed, who worked the late shift at one of the centre's stores. Because of the large number of customers in the store near closing time, he was running a little late to catch his bus for home. He was making a dash for the bus because it was the last one for the night when the officer stopped him. He questioned Warren at length as to why he was there and, even after an answer that a Neanderthal would understand, insisted on checking his empty lunch bag after he noticed the bus was leaving. The officer kept him back on purpose until the bus had left, then laughed and told him, "I guess you'll have to walk home now long hair!" And he drove away laughing.

My daughter Alison's boyfriend was a young college student from Burlington, who managed to get a summer job at Wendy's. We invited him to stay here, and he often worked the early shift at the fast-food restaurant only a few blocks away. I let him use my old 2005 Chevy, as he had proved to be a responsible driver and I rarely went out. He had been stopped twice by police officers for no apparent reason and they had made him late for his shift. The third time he was stopped, he phoned me and we went to the location he had been stopped at. There was Josh, wearing a Wendy's uniform, hat, and name tag, being grilled by an older overweight, sloppy-looking policeman. There was no traffic at all, except us on the road, as there usually wasn't along the Lakeshore. I asked the officer if Josh was speeding, he replied no and had stopped him because he might have been driving a stolen car. When I asked for "any at all" reasonable explanation to stop an old car with a driver obviously going to work less than a block away at the Wendy's and who had given the proper address and owner of the car, the jerk (I use that because I am more sensitive) said to my face, "I checked and the car belongs to an old broad." I wonder if these officers have ever wondered why they are never in line for a promotion.

When we lived in a house close to the centre of Oshawa, Alison and a friend often went out in the evening to see a show or get a bite to eat. One evening, on the way home, they were accosted by a group of young thugs, who started pushing the girls and demanding money. The girls ran to the Oshawa police station, which literally was a few feet away, and ran into the main entrance asking for help. One officer was at the desk, and he said he was alone and couldn't help. He showed them the back door to the station, so they wouldn't be seen by the troublemakers still out front.

So much for serve and protect!

We live in a nice neighbourhood in South Oshawa. It's a small subdivision with single family homes. We have had numerous car break-ins, obviously by teenagers because they don't take any of my fifties music CDs but leave a mess, presumably looking for cash. One early morning, when I glanced out the window, I saw my passenger car door wide open. There had been a light snowfall and I could see footprints from my neighbour's car (also broken into) to my car (he probably ran when our security lights came on), down our driveway, and straight to the neighbour across the road's front door, where there lived a teenager old enough to quit school, stay in bed until two p.m., and generally cause trouble. I phoned the police because we finally had proof as to who was doing the break-ins: "Follow the prints!" I asked if they would help by sending an officer over, but she replied that everyone was too busy, and by the time they were available, the snow would probably have melted! I did approach the teen's mother and asked her if any of her cars had been damaged because the footprints, I explained, led right to her house. I think she got my message because they kicked their son out a few weeks later.

My volunteer identification for the Durham police Department

A few years ago, there was a write up in the local newspaper begging for police volunteers. As I was retired, I applied, thinking "If I can't beat them, I'll join them." I was fingerprinted, checked by Interpol, and had to supply numerous recommendations. I was then given a T shirt and volunteer police license to become assigned to the "puppet patrol." There was a small group of college students working for the summer, and with the help of gigantic Muppet-like puppets (I was the grandma puppet), we travelled a couple of times a week throughout the region to meet with groups of Brownies, Cub Scouts, daycare centres, and such to teach the children lessons, like "stranger danger" and what to do about dirty needles laying around, using the "voices" of the puppets and gestures. I thought it was a worthwhile safety and learning tool. As school started up again, I guess the students were no longer available. I phoned several times to offer my services but got no reply. So much for needing volunteers!

Part 3: Hospitals

Generations ago, there were definitely less hospitals, but more people didn't survive the numerous illnesses due to less knowledge and understanding. When we were children, the family doctor made house calls to serve the community and only severe illnesses were transferred to the local hospital. House calls went by way of the dodo bird, and medical clinics opened up, with sometimes hours and hours of wait time to see a physician. Not all clinics had extended hours, so invariably emergency rooms in our hospitals have become overcrowded. If you weren't ill when you were admitted, there was a good chance you would now leave with someone else's germs.

A couple of years ago, I had to go to the Oshawa General Hospital, renamed Lakeridge Health, Oshawa, because I had been vomiting for two straight weeks, unable to keep food and even any water down. As it was the supper hour, the waiting room was actually nearly empty, a very unusual occurrence for this emergency room. A very young doctor was on duty and a couple of nurses at the nursing station. I saw the triage nurse at the entrance, whose job is to assess each patient in order to determine the seriousness of each new admittance. She did the usual inquiries of temperature, BP, questions of symptoms, including if I suffered a headache. I told her I had a very low-grade headache due to the constant retching and vomiting, but that was all. After waiting over an hour while the young doctor shared coffee preferences and vacation locations with an attractive nurse, he glanced at my triage report and ordered a brain scan. He instructed a person, whom I don't known was cleaning services or actual medical staff, to escort me and my daughter to x-ray.

I was having difficulty walking due to extreme weakness and being held up by Alison, trying to follow the staff lead. She must've been in a hurry because she took off down the hall and disappeared. Alison was able to get directions to x-ray from some passerby, and we eventually arrived at our destination. After the required test, we return to the waiting room where a few more patients had accumulated. One was an elderly man, obviously suffering a form of dementia, shuffling around the waiting room, picking up soiled and used medical gloves that lay on the floor, and actually trying to put them on. The young doctors and nurses were busy talking and flirting and seemed totally oblivious to their surroundings. A family sitting next to me gently remove the gloves from the old gentleman and threw them into the garbage can. After another hour of waiting, the doctor had received the results from the brain scan and told Alison she could take me home because he assessed that I didn't have a brain tumour! No blood work was taken at the time. Two days later, my condition deteriorated even more: I was hallucinating, unable to walk or talk sensibly, or really be aware of my surroundings. My family doctor told Alison to take me back to the hospital and refuse to leave until the doctor on duty ordered blood work and actually pretended how to be a medical professional. I remember very little of this visit, but I do recall that I was lucky enough to have the same incompetent young doctor. Alison angrily yelled at him and gave him the advice that our family doctor had said. He said to Alison after she reeled him out, "Well, she didn't look this crummy the last time!"

I have, unfortunately, being required to visit the emergency room on a number of occasions, owing to an ongoing illness for the last fifteen years. Usually, the doctors on call are extremely efficient and of the highest caliber, but I believe the hospital seems to have a problem on occasion in finding competent personnel to "man the ship" so to speak.

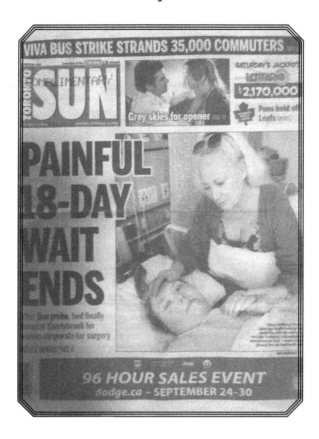

The Toronto Sun front page

One such occasion was when Alison was involved in a catastrophic accident. The car that she was a passenger in was broadsided by a truck whose driver, a young man, made an illegal turn. Luckily, the accident occurred at a main intersection where the police were enjoying a break at a café (dare I say, "Doughnut shop") and was able to call for an ambulance immediately. I arrived at the Oshawa Hospital shortly after she was admitted. Alison was screaming in pain, and a nurse said the doctor would have to see her before she could administer anything to relieve the pain. A female EMS sat at the nursing station, her feet on the desk, eating an apple, yelling for Alison to "shut up" because nothing could be done for her until the doctor saw her.

I caught a fleeting glance of a doctor a few times. He was very elderly and became very busy when an obese man came into emergency, complaining of chest pain, which started in the restaurant where he was dining. The doctor decided *he* had to do an ECG right away in case of a heart attack, instead of letting a nurse perform this test. On his way to attend Alison, a drunk entered the ER. He had fallen through a plate glass window and the doctor decided he needed immediate attention. Meanwhile the EMS continued to yell at Alison while she screamed in pain. I felt so completely helpless, frustrated, and angry. Eventually, the doctor managed to order an x-ray and give her some relief.

She required extensive surgery, which apparently couldn't be done in Oshawa, and after eighteen days of agony and nothing accomplished, I phoned the *Toronto Sun* to explain the entire circumstances and incompetence. I had run home briefly to phone and feed the dog, and when I returned to the hospital, I found the room full of reporters and photographers. They demanded action and went to the hospital director to demand something be done. That night, Alison was transferred to a Toronto hospital and had major surgery the following day. Thank goodness for the *Toronto Sun!*

When I was caring for my parents, Dad had not been feeling quite well. When they moved to Oshawa, I found a doctor at a clinic taking new patients. She was East Indian and Dad was delighted because he spoke Urdu and had spent years in India. Unfortunately, she went back to India on a holiday and never returned. Therefore, I had to take him to emergency when he was feeling ill.

He spent two days in the hallway at Oshawa before being transferred to a bed upstairs. They put him into a semi room at the end of the hall, furthest from the nursing station. The other bed was empty, so he was alone and basically forgotten. They had put a catheter in him because the nurses had said he couldn't see where the bathroom was due to his blindness and put his side rails up. He couldn't find the call bell, didn't know if it was night or day, couldn't reach a jug of water on his bedside table, and couldn't see anyway, and the kitchen staff brought his meals to the table on the empty bed next to him. They would return later in remark, "Oh, aren't you hungry?" He wasn't washed or shaved, and I ended up coming in three times a day to meet all his needs.

One day, a doctor with an entourage came to his room. He was a gastroenterologist (I am familiar with him and, if I am being nice, would call him an ignorant pig) and announced to Dad, "I am going to do a colonoscopy." Dad said, "What's that?" This (I'm being nice) jerk said, "I take a garden hose and shove it up your ass!" I was so shocked, and the idiot's followers said nothing. Dad just said, "You are not!" Then the group left. I discharged Dad immediately and took him home. I removed the catheter, as it was only used because of the hospital laziness. No one, absolutely no one, should be subjected to some of the behaviour I have observed at Oshawa, in spite of the most excellent physicians that may get a bad reputation due to the incompetency of others. I wonder if this is possibly due to the fact that area hospitals now come under "Lakeridge Health" organization—a case, perhaps like the long-term care homes, where they are in the business of making money while providing less care, fewer real professionals, and less services. Just a thought!

Ancestry

The Forgans

Grandpa is the youngest Forgan on the far right

Gaga- Beautiful young lady

Gaga as a teenager

Grandpa, Gaga, Uncle Dae, and Mom

The Jacks

Robert Jack – far right as a youngster

Grandpa Robert Jack as an infant with his parents and brother Wilson

Granny with her three boys: Wilson, Jimmy, and Robert

David, Mom, Dad, Diana, and me

David in full uniform of the Black Watch Regiment

Me – in 2000

The four generations: Grandpa, me, Mom and Robbie

Epilogue

Old Age?

With the passing of time, the body and mind start to slow down. Our bones stiffen and occasionally creak, our memory fades, wrinkles appear, our skin sags, and generally, our health suffers. It is a tedious process, but denial often helps. I always said, "I don't have wrinkles; they are laugh lines." However, now when I glance gingerly in a mirror, I realize my face says I must find everything hysterical! Getting down to grass level to do a little gardening is a task in itself. I now avoid it since the time a neighbour spied me crawling over our driveway. I claimed I had lost something when in reality I was trying to reach table, chair, or tree so I could haul myself up to a standing position. My short-term memory fully escapes me. I am a fan of criminal TV shows—help me if I am ever pulled into an interrogation room for questioning in a criminal case! The proverbial detective would ask me what I was doing and where a month ago on a Thursday evening. For heaven's sake, I don't remember what day it is today or even what I had for breakfast this morning.

I have taken to using the great invention of "sticky notes." I have them all over the house to remind me of what to do, where to do it, and when. Unfortunately, having a phone number on the little square piece of paper beside the phone doesn't help if I have forgotten to include the name and why I had to phone said person. The handiest tool in my kitchen is my timer. I am in the habit of cooking hard boiled eggs for my husband's lunches and use the timer to remind me they are boiling on the stove. My kitchen ceiling is a testament of my forgetfulness. There are tiny pieces of eggshells and telltale bits of eggs firmly stuck to the plaster as proof of my neglect at not remembering to press the "on" button on the timer.

Right now most of my long-term memory is intact. At least if I lose it entirely, I can always read the book about my life. If only I can remember the author's name!

Dorothy F. Hart

CPSIA information can be obtained
at www.ICGtesting.com
Printed in the USA
BVHW071206050921
616048BV00004B/40